PREACHING THAT MAKES THE WORD PLAIN

Preaching That Makes the Word Plain

Doing Theology in the Crucible of Life

William Clair Turner Jr.

CASCADE *Books* • Eugene, Oregon

PREACHING THAT MAKES THE WORD PLAIN
Doing Theology in the Crucible of Life

Copyright © 2008 William Clair Turner Jr. All rights reserved. Except for brief quotations in critical publications or reviews, no part of this book may be reproduced in any manner without prior written permission from the publisher. Write: Permissions, Wipf and Stock Publishers, 199 W. 8th Ave., Suite 3, Eugene, OR 97401.

Cascade Books
A Division of Wipf and Stock Publishers
199 W. 8th Ave., Suite 3
Eugene, OR 97401

www.wipfandstock.com

ISBN 13: 978-1-55635-586-8

Cataloging-in-Publication data:

Turner, William Clair, 1948–
    Preaching that makes the word plain : doing theology in the crucible of life / by William Clair Turner Jr.

    xvi + 114 p.; 23 cm.

    ISBN 13: 978-1-55635-586-8

    1. Preaching. I. Title.

BV4211.2 .T89 2008

Manufactured in the U.S.A.

CONTENTS

Introduction vii

PART I   Conceiving the Task

one   Preaching That Makes the Word Plain 3

two   From Scribble to Script: A Spirituality of Preaching 20

three   Nuts and Bolts: A How-To Guide for Preachers 29

PART II   The Practice of Preaching

four   The Word of Faith 59

five   Going to the Outer Limits 66

six   The Suppressed Side of Christmas 73

seven   Riches from the Manger 79

eight   Emancipating the Proclamation 86

nine   Tidings of Good Things 92

ten   The Work of Faith 99

eleven   The Good News of Divine Provocation 106

Bibliography 113

INTRODUCTION

Nearly twenty-five years ago, not long after completing my doctoral work, Dr. C. Eric Lincoln, who chaired my committee, suggested that I write a book entitled, "Why I Preach." He said there should be an introduction about preaching, followed by a collection of sermons. I could not see it then, as I had just completed the dissertation and was looking to launch a scholarly project. He saw what I could not see. Preaching is my passion. For me it is the seminal interaction between the living God through the scriptures, embodied in one who lives among the people of God.

Coming through the civil rights, black power, and Vietnam War eras forced upon me the issues of prophetic critique and ministry that is relevant to the cries of the oppressed. It is fair to say that the theological critique prompted by these movements is what permitted my continuing embrace of the Christian faith. The themes of those times reinforced the centrality of the gospel and the power of the Christian pulpit (for good and for ill). The strengths and weaknesses of the church pivot on the interrelationship between theology as a critical discipline and the dispensation of the gospel in the crucible of life. It is the dispensation that shapes the lives of persons and communities as faithful witnesses to the Son of God, or fashions imposters that bring shame to the name of Messiah Jesus.

The intervening years have been punctuated by an active schedule of preaching and teaching in the areas of theology, black church studies, homiletics, and ministry. The exercise has been one that is characterized by tension. Indeed, it fits the description Jacob gave for Issachar when he blessed his sons—namely, the blessing of being balanced by two burdens. There is the burden of preaching to the people of God, hearing their cries, and carrying them before God. Then there is the burden of teaching others how to do the work of ministry. For me there has been balancing grace to fight against the tilt toward unreflective ministry on the one hand, and teaching and research not grounded in the life of the church on the other.

An administrative appointment in Black Church Affairs opened latitude in teaching not afforded while on a tenure track in theology. While under that appointment an opportunity arose to shift into homiletics and ministry. The result was that the practices of ministry became the focus for my ongoing interests in pneumatology and the critical study of the African American church. It opened the way for me to teach what I practice, and to probe the practices of ministry as content (text) for reflection.

Along with reading texts on preaching, teaching preaching, and doing the work of preaching, I have taken time to reflect on some of the preachers who had foundational impact on me. At the time I had no clue regarding how their spiritual fingerprints were being used of God to shape a malleable lump of clay. On occasions it is as though I can hear their voices in the background, carrying on a conversation over my shoulder as I do my work. It is like some sort of spiritual protoplasm, or formative DNA has been left with me like a mystical residue, leaving a sense (*sensus*) for how to listen to the word for the sake of having something to say to the people. It is as though I ask the question raised within myself more than forty years ago, namely, how did they go from that text to that sermon? Below is a Short Roll Call.

James Forbes came to pastor my home church (St. John's United Holy Church of America, Richmond, Va.) while I was a teenager. Excitement filled the air and the church wherever he preached or spoke for any reason. It was nothing short of amazing what this young, brilliant, theologically trained Pentecostal preacher could do with a text, and how he could make the pulpit come to life like his predecessors. He made you want to listen to him, but even more, listen to the text. He could take the old traditions of the church, find the doctrinal and scriptural roots, and breathe new life into them. He had a gift for making the word oh-so-relevant—contemporary, fresh, and insightful. In his hands, preaching was far more than prohibitions, and hellfire, which was fairly standard for holiness-Pentecostal preaching of that day. Later I learned how the content was culled out by meticulous exegesis and refracted through the theology of Paul Tillich and Karl Barth—to name two of the more prominent theologians of the mid twentieth century. This was true of many seminary trained black preachers in the latter third of the twentieth century.

We had heard his father. A former pastor, Bishop W. M. Clements, would invite him to preach revivals and for other special occasions. Clements called him Professor Forbes, and when he came the place was buzzing with great anticipation. Forbes the elder preached in a clear and powerful way that could not be forgotten. Forbes the younger joined with other luminaries of Richmond during that era. The list includes Samuel Proctor (who imprinted a generation), Robert Taylor, Y. B. Williams, David Shannon, Paul Nichols, and others whose names need to be enshrined for posterity.

The time was the sixties. We had heard from Martin Luther King Jr. and those prophetic strains could not be dismissed from our ears. More, we had heard from Malcolm X as well.[1] He was insightful, critical, analytical, and compelling as an orator. The only problem was that we didn't hear enough from him about Jesus, and we could not reconcile Adam with Yacub. For me the preaching of Forbes was like a prescription. It was most appealing and critical in opening space for a teenage lad to remain in the church with a Christian option to Malcolm.

Then there was Miles Jones. He came to Richmond in the sixties as well, and he pastored in the community where we lived (Providence Park). Never could a man do so much with the word! He could take a word given in the text and examine it, cross-examine it, look into it, listen to it, and wait for it to yield treasures. The question with which I was left on a constant basis was, "How in the world did he get so much out of a word we all had heard so many times?" The patience with which the work was done was astounding. There was not the "moan" or the tune that was standard for older preachers and often heard from younger ones as well. The preaching was full of inspiration and packed with information. And some of the people would still shout.

A man came from Brooklyn to install Miles Jones. He was not known around town before he came. But those who heard him never forgot him. So clear was his presentation, so forceful were his words, so relevant were his applications. His was preaching that was refreshing beyond measure.

---

1. As college students we listened to both Martin Luther King Jr. and Malcom X on 33LP records. The social analyses of both were amazingly close. There was a toss-up between them when it came to their oratory. Malcolm was every bit the "fiery preacher," who possessed enormous persuasive gifts for moving an audience.

It took us a while to get it, but the name of the man was Sandy Ray (The Reverend Dr.). And we understood better why Miles preached the way he did.

Philip Cousin, a young pastor in Durham, was a rising star in the African Methodist Episcopal Church, who later was elected a bishop. I attached myself to him as a college student and later as a seminarian. He was insightful, polished, full of knowledge and inspiration. His preaching was charged with contemporary relevance. He was astute to the tenor of the times, and his involvement as an activist was a mirror on the word he proclaimed. Actually, he taught me the only "formal" course I ever took in preaching, and he also taught black theology at Duke University Divinity School.

In him was a distillation of African Methodism. This theological tradition was populated with names I had never heard. Names like Richard Allen, Daniel Payne, Henry Turner, Reverdy Ransom. Cousin represented the tradition of preaching that was bursting forth under the nomenclature of black theology. Indeed, from the outset black theology was the essence of reading the scriptures through the interpretive lens of the African American pulpit.

The fingerprints of the black church that are all over the seminal statements coming from the National Committee of Negro Churchmen (later National Committee of Black Churchmen) were antecedently on him. This theology had roots that went deep into the soil and soul of the black independent church movement of the 1900s. It was tethered to the activism that birthed the church's investment in abolition, emancipation, and the twentieth-century struggle for social justice. This preaching oozed with the passions (yea, the harmonies) of liberty, and was wedded to the strong and unapologetic call for conversion. Later I learned that this synthesis was at the very root of the faith into which I was born and from which I drew natal nurture.

A. W. Lawson influenced me as the quintessential churchman, whom I watched preach for the nurture, building, development, and molding of a congregation and a connectional church (the United Holy Church of America). I spent five years under his tutelage following the completion of my MDiv at Duke. A man full of wisdom, he exegeted within the tension of the worlds converging inside him. But more, he had a keen sense for where the church was being carried by the Spirit. A bishop in the United Holy Church of America with uncommon prescience, his intention was to join the power of the pulpit to a theology of the Spirit that moved it beyond the constrictions of fundamentalism and experiential dogmatism.

Bishop Lawson possessed uncommon theological sense for reading out what was given in the text to the destination embodied in living, breathing Christian communities. He was able to make doctrine come to life in a manner that was neither shallow nor denominationally limited. He stood in a tradition of great but lesser known preachers like H. L. Fisher, J. D. Diggs, G. J. Branch, E. B. Nichols, and J. W. Houston.[2] While being "the theologian" of the United Holy Church, he was also the teacher and mentor for a vast number of young preachers in Durham and from various church traditions in eastern North Carolina. The influence remains strong within churches that were influenced by these pastors who still credit him for their initial studies, and the grounding he supplied in the practical wisdom (*phronesis*) that gives guidance and stability to the church.

It was from serving as his assistant that I was introduced to the wonderful discipline of *lectio continua*. We would select a book from which to preach and listen to what the writer had to say for a sustained period. Normally we preached from the Old Testament in the fall (an extended Advent), the gospels from the first of the year (Epiphany and Lent), and from an epistle following Easter (Easter, Pentecost, and Ordinary Time). It is from this seminal, life-giving, mutual interpenetration between the word and the life of God's people that good preaching emerges. This is the humus of pulpit theology that must remain as the anchor of the church, and the vital interlocutor for all other discourses that claim to do any reasoning about God.

When I went to the administrative track I felt free to teach what was in my heart. I never stopped preaching regularly for any significant period of time. First I taught an elective course in preaching. It was fun, and it seemed to go well. Eventually I taught the required course, to fill some gaps in coverage. That turned into an even more exciting venture as well.

Nearly twenty-five years later I have come back to the point suggested by the sage C. Eric Lincoln. Along the way there have been numerous points in the pilgrimage that have proved essential for the task. Without

---

2. See Turner, *United Holy Church of America*.

these stations I could scarcely give an account that would be clear to me or intelligible to anyone else. It is only in the crucible of preaching with regularity, and teaching in the fields listed above, that enough mist has lifted to understand and talk about this challenging work. And there is every hope to understand it even better bye and bye.

The distant background for my reflection on preaching (which informs my teaching) is the emergence of the black theology project in the second half of the twentieth century. There one can see the beginning stages of theology as an academic project rooted in the life of the church. It is a stage at which the church "lifts the voices" of those who do its reflective work and keeps them in a dialogue of mutual accountability. To be sure, this is not a moment without parallel in the long history of the church. But it is a moment deserving special notice in the American church.

This moment is one in which the church demanded to be heard—not just the church whose structures overlapped with those of the state, not only the church whose priests were approved by the king, but the church of former slaves, sharecroppers, and wage earners. Official theological tomes were rejected where they did not heed the God of the oppressed, follow the Lord who preached good news to the poor, and walk in the Spirit who gives liberty. The norm that emerged was the tension that required that if the voice of the academy deserves to be heard, it must see the interests of suffering humanity and hear from those who proclaim good news to the poor at every point. My quest as a preacher, a teacher of preaching, and a homiletical theologian is to privilege the tension as the methodological starting point and set it at the center of the practice of preaching as theological practice.

Essentially the method of black theology in its inception is what Henry Mitchell reiterated in *Black Preaching*. With an explicit interest in preaching, he looked at the thought of African American preachers, as Benjamin Mays did previously in his classic study, *The Negro's God as Reflected in His Thought*. The same trajectory is followed for the sake of doing ethics in Peter Paris' *The Social Teachings of the Black Churches*. In other words, for groundbreaking work in systematics, preaching, and ethics there is a return to the same source. Close attention was given to how the African American Church (with the pulpit at the center) read the bible and reflected on the meaning of its life in God.

Knowledge of God from the scriptures—refracted through the experience of oppression, suffering, and triumph—was the standpoint in judgment from which to critique the formal theologies, especially those that served the ends of bondage rather than liberation. This work was not done outside of conversation with others doing theology, especially those of like mind. But discriminating taste was used to fashion a norm by which to know what was "a trick of the devil" under the guise of theology.

I am reminded here of what Howard Thurman said of his grandmother, who could not read herself, but would not allow him to read from Paul. In her judgment the slave-owners construction of texts instructing slaves to obey their masters was not consistent with the God she had come to know. Indeed, she was so bold as to question whether any such passage was in the bible at all.

Along with the skill for how to interpret the scriptures is the "sense for how to preach." The question is how to deliver the word so that it has life and power. But alas, this sense for how to preach is not separable from how to read the scriptures. Reading and interpreting the scriptures for the sake of preaching is more than a technical exercise in exegesis.

One might even go so far as to employ the term coined in some circles as "interpretating the bible."[3] That is the employment of the "sanctified imagination" in the acts of reading, meditating, seeing into, and "chewing the scroll." It is "tasting to see," it is "seeing the voice," it is being "touched by the fire" of the word. The sense here is that one must see and feel something before having anything to say that is worth hearing. The word is no dead letter; it is spirit and life. One could even hear the old preachers say at a point in the sermon, "I see something here." Or, they would call upon a character from the scriptures as a witness—e.g., "Come here John, and tell me what you see."

The sense of preacher as one who sees and hears is taken up in the oracles transcribed in J. W. Johnson's *God's Trombones*. The prayer for the preacher was that God would "Pin his ear to the wisdom-post, / . . . Put his eye to the telescope of eternity, / . . . turpentine his imagination," so that his words might be "sledgehammers of truth."[4]

---

3. In some cases this was but a mispronunciation of the word "interpretation." But in other cases it reflected the engagement of the "sanctified imagination" that allowed the preacher to look into the word.

4. Johnson, *God's Trombones*, 14.

Now the question is, how do you write about—and more, teach—such an art form so that there is integrity in the word that is being declared? I can recall oh-so-clearly the conviction that came upon me for the short-lived effort to sacrifice the content for the style during a period when I believed I did not have time for all the preparation I was led to give to the sermon. The consequence was colossal failure that was obvious to me first of all. I can only assume how painful it was for those who listened.

These are the "methodological currents" that go into my reflections on preaching. They are not contrary to other formal statements concerning preaching found in the standard texts. But these texts do not get to the heart of the project as I have experienced it being done. How shall I say it? They are good for what they are and what they do. But something goes on in the Black Pulpit that is well nigh mystical. I could expand this to all pulpits that are alive with vitality.

Writing about preaching reminds me of the conversation between the angel and the captive beside the river in Babylon. The captive had serious questions regarding the suffering of Israel, and he wanted some answers. After much of the evasion of the angel (or so the captive thought) the angel came back with questions of his own. He asked the captive to measure a pound of fire, a bushel of wind, to call back a day that was past, and make visible the shape of a human voice. Then he would give the explanation.

O preacher, how do you do your work? Take me into your workshop, into the workspace. Let me in on the secrets. Methodologically speaking, this sort of question is what I am seeking to probe. It honors but does not accept fully the old wisdom that the art of preaching is "caught rather than taught," or that it is "better felt than tellt."

In the not so distant background is my memory of the anguish of black preachers in the generation that preceded me. Some died and others still live with a strong degree of regret for loosing the talent they took to seminary and being trained away from their people. Studying preaching requires taking the risk of coming out sounding like your teacher. Well into the seventies and beyond, white churches would not call a black preacher, and black churches would not have you if you could not preach with an acceptable delivery.

Equally well, I remember the general anxiety of African American congregations over subscribing to a Duke-trained African American preacher. A person (or congregation) had no idea what they might be getting. Shaw, Virginia Union, Hood, Gammon, and other black seminaries and colleges had been training ministers as part of their original mission, and their track records were clear. But what would a Duke-trained black preacher do? To put it politely, there was fear.

I will ever remember the scene following preaching to the Hampton mini-conference. A Baptist preacher rattled his jaws and said, ". . . You didn't learn that at Duke." On another occasion I preached for an AME Conference. The bishop "put me up . . . to see what the young doctor could do." The Lord blessed a sermon entitled, "The Power of God's Approval." Some time later that day one of the younger preachers commented, "Now I'm not scared to go to Duke anymore." Methodologically speaking, I am seeking to set forth a way of doing the work by which I have sought to prepare preachers to be effective dispensers of the word with careful regard (not disregard) for the communities from which they come and to which they will be called or sent.

In the foreground is the need to serve a generation who did not hear the elders and whose experiences are so different that it is hard to appreciate how they did their work. In the view of many, the criteria for good preaching are set by media and consumer appeal. Dominant themes for this preaching are prosperity, wealth, patriotism, and material blessing. The primary vendors tend to be academic theologians who write for each other, or self-proclaimed popular theologians who are not subject to structures of accountability.

The busy preacher can easily become the consumer of theologies that take on the guise of scientific scholarship, or that boast of not being theology at all. The underlying interest in this effort is the quest for recovering the pulpit as an arena in which responsible theology is done as source and interlocutor with the widest possible public. I do believe that is what my esteemed teacher had in mind.

Part I consists of methodological discussions that reflect on preaching as the necessary work that must be done by persons who would speak faithfully for God. Revelation and inspiration notwithstanding, human hands must be set to tasks that demand great effort.

Chapter 1 explores theological tensions in preaching that reach all the way into exegesis. Because preaching is to be understood, it can never be free of tethers that connect it to the texts that give authority, and to the times and seasons during which it is uttered. An effort is made to show how work done with integrity honors the source and destination of preaching.

Chapter 2 sets the preacher in pneumatic space—space saturated by the Spirit. The location is somewhere between art and skill, between the mystical sphere in which the word is received and the mundane tasks like scratching the papyrus or striking the keyboard. This is where tedious tasks are sanctified. An attempt is made to say with words how hard work is turned into holy habits, so that one can grow to cherish the chores of preaching.

Chapter 3 is a discussion of the mechanics involved in putting a sermon together. It identifies knowledges from which good preaching draws so they can be set in place for the necessary homiletical judgments that must be made.

Part II is a selection of sermons preached from Romans 10, which is itself a mini-treatise on preaching. The sermons illustrate the methods discussed in Part I. They are transparent to the data of life in a particular Christian community. They advance the discussion of what preaching is and how it is done by refracting the word given in specific texts through the rhythms of life.

Join me, if you will, through the pages under this cover in my quest for a wedding between "teaching what I practice," and "practicing what I teach."

PART I Conceiving the Task

one PREACHING THAT MAKES THE WORD PLAIN

The essential nature of Christian preaching cannot be overstated, no matter how many times the articulation is made. It is God's appointed means to proclaim redemption for the world. It has pleased God through the foolishness of preaching to save those who believe. Faith comes by hearing the word of God, but for there to be hearing, there must be a preacher. By preaching the church has lived; by preaching she is revived. Though archaic in form, no adequate replacement has been found. By now those who would embark upon such a quest should well be weary of their failed effort.

Concerns for understanding, clarity, relevance, and concreteness sound all but tautological in the matter of preaching. It is God's address to particular human creatures, at a particular time, and under particular circumstances. This is not to say that no factors pertaining to preaching are timeless, or that one generation cannot benefit from the truth deposited in a preceding one. But it is given with the very nature of preaching that it be contemporary, relevant, and pointed accurately at the environment in which it is uttered.

Preaching makes Christ present among the people. The ether in which it thrives is the life of worship within a doxological and obedient community. It is given power by the very breath of God. It is spoken into huddled and fearful masses; it calls men and women from their idols; it encourages the faith of those who have believed; it witnesses to the work of the Father and the completion of all things in the Son that the creation may be a habitation of God in the Spirit. Indeed, one would do well to question an utterance offered as preaching if it is not fresh, relevant, and understood.

Preaching Is to Be Understood

The notion of *Preaching to be Understood* is probably not articulated better than in a book by James Cleland that bears that name.[1] Dean of the chapel at Duke University in the sixties, he had the unenviable task of preaching to college students in a rebellious generation. But, wonder of all wonders, he was one of the few in his era who could pull off that chore—namely, filling the chapel. On the surface was the charm of a man who looked like a leprechaun, and accompanying that pose was a thick Scottish brogue. But below the surface was a notion of preaching that is all but obvious: it is to be understood. The visual image he gave to press that notion into the imagination of the developing preacher is the geometrical shape known as an ellipse.

Rather than having a center like the circle, the ellipse has two foci. One of the foci is the text of scripture, the other is the contemporary situation (or the context).[2] Together they portend the circumference of the ellipse, which Cleland called the preached word. It is not to be confused with the "read word"; neither is it to be confused with the word of prophecy that comes by direct revelation. There is interpenetration between the two texts, and it occurs in the person of the preacher, who is one from among the people. By its very nature, preaching is a hermeneutical act: it translates; it makes relevant; it puts truth into context; it makes the word of God concrete.

Cleland introduced the notion of "bifocality" to describe this model. His position is that no matter where one is located along this circumference, what one has is the word. What I want to press here is how the passion to be understood translates into methodological questions in the work of exegesis. That is, how does one exegete both within tension, and with intention? This is the task to which I now want to turn with undivided attention.

Exegeting Within Tension

All reading and exegeting of scripture is within the tension of an utterance that is at once for God and for the people. Gardner Taylor makes

---

1. Cleland, *Preaching to be Understood*.
2. See Cleland's chapter on "bifocal preaching," 33–58.

much of the audacity of the creature to speak for God, who is everlasting, holy, the creator.[3] And yet, with nothing to say for God, the preacher has nothing worth listening to as preaching. Preachers are not isolated selves, mere Cogitos who know their existence through thinking. No, preachers have feet of clay. Preachers are human, frail, and flawed. They dwell among people of unclean lips, and they know it. Preachers eat cornbread and watermelon, navy beans and rice, fried chicken and catfish, sweet potatoes and collard greens. And yet they stand in the divine counsel and tremble as they hear from heaven. Or, they proceed to speak without hearing and tremble at the prospect of their own judgment. They know the blood of the lost is required at their hands if they do not speak; and they know the hearer may well demand their blood when they do utter what God gives.

The first thing that must be said about exegeting within tension is that there is tension within the "spine" of every sermon. In this regard the sermon differs from the mere telling of a biblical story, the narrating of selected verses, or a personal testimony. Because of this tension inherent within the sermon, reflection, analysis, and design are to a sermon what the backbone is to a living creature that is able to stand up and walk. The thesis makes a claim about God from within a tradition of faith that has specific consequences for those who hear. The challenge might be the call to repent. It may be a summons to deepen faith by growing in knowledge or appropriating what is known. It may be a rebuke for disobedience, a clarification of the distinction between the word of the Lord and the word of the land. The claim may be to compel obedience and service, but the consequences are always present. The spine distributes the thought throughout the discourse, making obvious why what is said is more than the opinion of the preacher.

The tension—just as the spine does for the human body—makes the sermon a discourse toward which there cannot be indifference. By means of it a sermon can be reduced to its skeleton—its summary, its points, its moves. Tension is what makes it hold together and stick. Or, tension is what makes it "snap back," so it can get up, go somewhere, get in the "grill," the business, in one's face or space. Preaching done within tension can convict, comfort, and console or it can motivate, enrage, empower,

---

3. Taylor, *How Shall They Preach*, 24.

and deliver. But it should not allow for claims of misunderstanding or indifference.

The second thing that must be said about preaching within tension is that Christian preaching, without exception, is grounded in the scriptures. The scriptures are the revealed written word of God. They are given by inspiration of God for doctrine, correction, and reproof. As the writer of 2 Peter puts it, "holy men of God" were moved by the Holy Ghost to make a record of what the Spirit inspired in them (2 Pet 1:19–21). The same Spirit illumines the mind of the preacher, yet the interpretation is not a private affair. It is done within tension: there is a community of interpretation (a *koinonia* of the Spirit) without which this work cannot be done, and there is a witness in those who are convicted and hear what the Spirit has to say to the church.

The word spoken in preaching is brought out of the scriptures. This work, known as "exegesis," is not to be confused with "eisigesis," which means *to read into*. Eisigesis occurs when we know before we consult the scriptures, or when we know the meaning of a text before taking the time to listen to the text as a subject with integrity. There is value in bringing out all that is given in a text for the sake of knowledge. But a tension is present in the task of preaching. What is brought *out of the text* for the purpose of preaching has a concrete focus given by the historicity of the text and the community to which it is spoken.

A critical element of tension is to be observed at this point. It occurs at the boundary between exegetical irrelevance and eisigesis. Exegetical irrelevance goes beyond the parameters observed by the written text into detail that has no bearing on the claim being made by God or for the people of God. Eisigesis disregards the claim in favor of the preacher's interest. The tension is located where the claim of the text confronts and engages the concrete issues and interests of those who hear preaching. In eisigesis the text is tortured to make it say what the preacher has predetermined. This occurs when we already know what we want to say and find "a word" in the text on which to hang it, or when we string together a set of texts to "flip and hop"—sometimes from Genesis to Revelation. The exegetical tension out of which empowered preaching emerges comes from waiting on the word we could not find without the disciplines of consecrated listening.

Such listening can be compared to the "tuning action" required for the old fashion radio and television. Before there was digital capacity, one had to turn a knob to get the true wave. When the tuning was not precise one would get static on the radio, or what looked like snow on the black and white television screen. Even when tuned, the dial would sometimes slip, and the static and snow would return. Consecrated listening is the first step toward encoding the speech of preaching so it strikes the listening ear with digital precision. We preach to a generation that does not desire to do the work of tuning.

The scriptures reveal who God is, who we are, and what we need to know. The tension in which preaching occurs pivots on the axiom that what we are given is what we need. The implication of preaching grounded in the scriptures is that there is a word in the given text—a word those who are present need to hear. The first work of the preacher is "tuning the ear" to hear with clarity. This is an immersion that may be called "synesthesia," in that there is a total participation in the "ether of the word" that cannot be reduced to a single sense. This is on the order of "tasting to see," "looking to hear," or "smelling to be touched." It is being handled by the word of life to know what to say to particular people.

Exegeting the scriptures for preaching is not to be reduced to the historical and critical methods developed in the nineteenth and twentieth centuries. They have their place, but they do not replace nearly twenty centuries of the church's exegetical work. Nor do these methods guarantee the healthy tension required for twenty-first-century preaching. They are good for what they were designed to do. They identify the sources that feed into the books of the canon, showing parallels with other ancient literature. They identify the form of the literature, so we can distinguish one genre from another. Critical study exposes the institutions within ancient Hebrew culture, comparing it with customs of surrounding peoples. By means of these studies we learn the interconnections between what we now distinguish as religious teaching and practice, from political, economic, and social structures and patterns. Examining how the sources were edited serves to indicate the issues that were pressing for the compiler and help us to know the theology that operates in a given book. Language study is crucial for knowing the meaning of words in their origin, root meaning, and the world of images out of which they emerged. This component of exegesis is crucial, and it must never be set aside or diminished. But it must be kept in tension with other knowledges to serve the purposes of preaching.

If we are to preach within tension, we must also be attentive to the times and seasons in which we preach. Before the departure of the Lord at the end of his earthly ministry, the disciples asked Jesus whether the moment preceding his ascension was the time when he would restore the kingdom to Israel. His answer was that it was not for them to know the times and seasons the Father had reserved for his power. Rather, they would receive power after the Holy Ghost came upon him to be witnesses in Jerusalem, Judea, Samaria, and the utmost parts of the earth. The Lord did not say it was not for them to know the times and seasons in which they carried forth the ministry given to them, however. Indeed, the Spirit was given precisely so they might know their times and seasons.

The times and seasons of the text and the context must be exegeted for preaching to be focused and clear. For the text of scripture, the critical methods identified with biblical scholarship are indispensable. Along with them, however, come all of the theological disciplines, as well as the emancipating knowledges coming from the human sciences, and the critical knowledge of the natural sciences.

The manner in which the scriptures have been interpreted in the long history of the church is utterly consequential for preaching in the twenty-first century. Indeed, the dogmatic constructions of the church are the direct consequence of how the scriptures have been read. Doctrine did not fall from the sky. This is true both of the doctrines that unite Christians and those that divide them. To put the matter another way, there are no Christians who concede that their teaching is "unscriptural." What one finds in both the written and unwritten text of believing communities reflects the efforts of living, believing Christians to make sense of the scriptural deposit that has been received as well as those things believed and taught among them.

Dogmatics operate at the threshold of the faith. They deal with what must be believed and confessed for persons to claim they are Christian. Or they compel an account of how a claim can be made to Christian identity without such a confession. An outline of dogmatics follows the order of the statements of the creeds of the church. No matter what one's denomination, members do well to be familiar with these boundaries. Otherwise there can be great and costly forfeiture of troves of wisdom.

Systematics keep one mindful of what must be said to confess the mystery of godliness in a manner that is consistent and coherent. For example, systematics prevents a statement concerning the Spirit to contradict what must be said concerning the Son. Attention is given by this discipline to how what is said at one point in confession interpenetrates all else that must be said. In addition, systematics seek for coherence between theological knowledge and other fields that do not pretend to be driven by a search for understanding the knowledge of God that comes by faith.

Knowledge of times and seasons also penetrates into the thickness of concrete, historical Christian communities, known as denominational and nondenominational churches. This is theology that presses below the threshold of written texts into oral traditions, patterns, gestures, idioms, and astructural content that are given with the pulse of the people. In this tissue one finds "ersatz" (informal) dogma where claims are staked and given the valence of gospel, and elevated to the status of sin and salvation, life and death. By this knowledge churches grow, or they go the way of defunct institutions that preceded them. These are the sorts of issues one finds addressed directly in the epistles and indirectly in the gospels. It is in this tension between the text and context that issues are disclosed as the impediments to the gospel they really are, or as the false faith that is not recognize as such. In the New Testament church issues such as circumcision and division were viewed in this light.

Preaching cannot occur without knowledge of the times and seasons of those to whom one preaches. Herein lies one of the great challenges for twenty-first-century preachers born before or shortly after the midpoint of the twentieth century. Seismic shifts in knowledge divide the century into two epistemological domains. The explosion of technology and virtual communication creates two worlds within the same families and communities. But similar shifts also occurred in matters of politics, economics, race, gender, and other descriptors by which we categorize our civilization. At the epicenter of this seismic shift are the theological issues of liberation and pneumatology. Preaching without knowledge of times and seasons reduces to the rhetoric and elocution of centuries that are past.

The tension that ties preaching to the seasons of the liturgical year also supplies health. It keeps the people of God focused on salvation history, supplying marvelous occasions for teaching the faith. Around these concrete moments can be found unsurpassed occasions for rehearsing the gospel. As one moves from Advent to Christmas, to Epiphany, to Lent, Easter, Pentecost, and Whitsuntide, opportunities are supplied for declaring the wondrous deeds of God in the thickness of life and the specificity of the human condition.

Holidays, cultural events, and idiomatic practices likewise supply tension. In some cases the opportunity is afforded for saying why a cultural event is not to be confused with Christian celebration at all. Other events beg to be lifted above the sentimentality and narcissism of parochial indulgences. Church Anniversary, for instance, begs for some discussion of ecclesiology and mission. Mother's Day and Men's Day are occasions for addressing the vocation of Christians in ordinary time in light of our calling under God. Methodologically speaking, the posture is that of listening to hear what the word might speak to a particular people on a specific occasion. It is asking the text, "What have you to say to the children of God today?"

It is no less than amazing to see what the findings are when one operates within boundaries and tensions. This is an approach to preaching that does not rely on cleverness and innovation. It takes seriously the sense of preaching found in the early church. One delivers in preaching what has been received from the Lord. A dispensation has been given to the preacher; the consequence is woe for not preaching the gospel. Preaching is an act of contending for the faith once delivered to the saints, and in undertaking the task one need not rely on tales artfully spun. When all is said and done, the mandate is to preach the remission of sins. We are sent by the Son, even as the Father has sent the Son, and we are accompanied by the very breath of God.

Bringing the times and seasons to the text is nothing less than the methodological performance of the question asked of Jeremiah by a young king named Zedekiah. What is so interesting in that case is that the young king did not really want to hear what the older prophet (who had been a friend of his father) had to say. Yet the question is on target. Faced with the dilemma of a kingdom under siege, he asked, "Is there any word from the Lord?"

Methodologically speaking, the issue is how to beg for the word needed in the moment, and how to open discursive spaces for its entrance. The opening is a *tempus* through which the word pierces, penetrates, illumines, and challenges the context and empowers the hearer. The word itself is a manifestation of power (a kratophany). This is where the word comes alive. Some have the wonderful gift for telling stories, or giving illustrations. Others will wear their selves out looking for stories, telling lies, or taking stories of others as their own.

Many more will be helped (and far better) by learning to exegete to the core of the text. This is where words come to life, where one discovers a key lodged in minute details for unlocking the mysteries. Or, we might say that one sees into the mystery. By means of a "lithic imagination,"[4] we are invited to look into the dense, opaque stone and see what has been given. Such keys open both the text and the context. Then preaching is far less a chore than a delight. It is a report of what has been shown to eyes that previously were "holden." The "stranger" who joins us—as he did the two who walked to Emmaus—makes our world without him seem strange as the bread of life is broken.

Exegeting with Intention

Nobody reads the bible without interests of some sort. Even those who read it as literature, for pleasure, or to dispute it have some purpose in mind. This is even more the case for those who read it as sacred text. Indeed, the claim for the bible as word of God, authoritative writing, or any other designation that indicates privilege necessarily involves a theological act. The privilege the bible has among human creatures means that there is no ordinary reading. The intention to which we now have reference, however, refers more to the subject who reads or hears what is brought forth from the scriptures.

It is like leading the children to stand before the mountain where God spoke from the flames of Sinai. It is like the prophet making a direct address to the king, who is confused regarding who is the troubler of

---

4. I am borrowing this term from Charles Long to account for the moment in which one gives full attention to reality that cannot be readily dominated or dissected. See Long, *Significations: Signs, Symbols, and Images in the Interpretation of Religion*. Long describes the moment as looking into a rock. Hence the term "lithic," taken from *lithos*, Greek for rock. What is desired is "in the rock," not under it or behind it. The moment is akin to the one in which the sculptor sees in the rock the image that is to be brought forth. For preaching, this is like looking into the word (the text) and waiting for the insight that must be given—an insight that cannot be rushed.

Israel: the selfish scoundrel who should be put to death, or the finger that writes to break up the sacrilegious drinking party? Again, it is like the prophet telling the king he must die and then pronouncing that fifteen years have been added to his life. Exegeting with intention is bringing a brother into the presence of the Messiah who sees and knows him prior to the introduction. It is the *ephphatic* encounter that opens the deaf ear (as with the man whose ear was opened by the word of Jesus in Mark 7:34), or the *ergersistic* event, where the command to rise performs the work of obedience, which is like resurrection (as with the cripples in Luke 5:23 and John 5:8).

With intention, a specific word is spoken to specific persons to address specific issues. This is more than the truth in general—whether it be the truth of the scriptures or the truth about the human condition. Just as there can be exegetical excess from the investigation of the text, so it can be from the context. Exegesis with intention refers to the truth of the word being applied on the spot. It is more than a statement of the case, as with social scientific analysis, or social commentary such as one hears in rap and hip-hop. It is more than theological truism, such as is found in trite speech, like "all things work together for good" taken out of context.

Just as one must submit to the world and reality of the scripture to rightly divide the word (cf. 2 Timothy 2:15), so one must give the mind to know the "madness and folly" that resides in the heart of the hearer. This hermeneutical principle, articulated by the preacher in the book of Ecclesiastes, is the only real option for those desiring to be heard and understood, especially in a day of epistemological shifts. In the truly dense spaces where civilizations intersect and clash—where eras join and separate—canons are not always clear.

Vexation of the spirit cannot be avoided in relevant and powerful preaching. The business is not usual. The subjects are not predictable. A trip to the commentary does not comprehend the madness of racism, wars of preemption, and suicide bombing. Nor does it make sense out of ethnic cleansing, genocide, and patricide. The madness must be stared in the face for knowledge of what it is—with comments about what ought to be the case suspended—till one sees what makes it tick. Children do not join gangs and commit suicide for nothing, despite the protests of parents concerning "how good they have it." Put another way, we do not know the mind of the generation by doing all the talking ourselves.

Twenty-first-century preaching is to a generation that to a significant degree knows nothing of the farm. Many persons in our civilization have no sense of the work that is required to plant, cultivate, and harvest crops. Food is purchased at the market, or it is bought prepared and ready to eat. Similarly with other forms of technology: the younger generation has come to rely on them—without the memory of times that predate such innovations—as if conveniences and gadgets simply came with the world. No explanation of the physics of electricity, magnetism, or electronics is required. On the other hand, where scientific knowledge is present, it can readily become the measure for all claims that are trustworthy. Verifiability is thought to reside in the measurement of the senses. In a context such as this, preaching from the scriptures seems to rest on knowledge from a strange and distant world.

Because of this strangeness and distance, countless images, metaphors, and parables from the bible have no resonance. The epistemological discontinuities often go unrecognized. Common sense realism has flowered into full bloom. Add to this the perduring pragmatism that is driven deeply into the American landscape, and the consequence is that much of what the bible has to say about human nature has an odd sound. The world of the bible is strange and foreign.

A necessary intention of preaching, therefore, must be to expose the hearer of the gospel to his or her own subjectivity. Knowledge and exploration of the epistemological breaks is as crucial for the exegetical task as critical study of the text. To put the matter another way, preaching with intention requires what Charles Long has called "archaeology of the subject." This is an interrogation of what it means to be modern, postmodern, American, or whoever we know ourselves to be. But sincere communication also requires taking seriously how we are known by those we consider as the Other. An intersubjective connection is present in every act of effective preaching.

A cornerstone in the structure of modern knowledge is the dictum popularized by the philosopher Hegel, that the rational is the real. He spoke in concert with others who sought to push back the curtain of mystery and enlighten the world. Despite the benefits of scientific knowledge deriving from this epistemological shift, reality has never caught up to the dictum. It refuses to evolve fully from magic, to religion, to science. As with the solution to the quadratic equation, there is a set of factors in plenary reality that have a coefficient of "i." If imaginary, there is a section of reality that remains real, even when it does not fit into rational constraints.[5] To use the language of Rudolf Otto, the "numinous" is as real as the rational.[6]

Preaching necessarily embraces the numinous (pneumatic) factors. It is inspired by the Spirit. It is an invitation into the world of mystery, even as it enters into the mysteries of the human heart. To the extent that it remains in tension with the scriptures and remains consistent with the intention for which it is given, preaching employs the language of pneumatology. Indeed, in some ways this archaic discourse is consistent with what might be nominated as the "postmodern tendency" of the twenty-first century.

Concern to speak to the times and seasons prevents the preacher from becoming a ventriloquist dummy for the culture. For then the tension would be broken, forfeiting the energy and power of preaching. When the preacher acts as dummy, her lips move, but another supplies the thoughtful reflection. The word of the Lord is confused with the word of the king and the voice of the land, as in the day of Ahab and Jehosophat. Ahab refused to call Micaiah, saying he only spoke evil and never what he wanted to hear. But all the other prophets were under the spell of the lying spirit. They would send the people into a battle where God had promised no protection and victory.

The image of the ventriloquist dummy was riveted in my imagination one night while watching Ted Coppell. There was a discussion between Jesse Jackson and Jerry Falwell prior to the demise of Apartheid in South Africa. Falwell called Bishop Tutu a phony and proceeded to apologize for the regime that was in power. There was no hint on his part of a need for "Regime Change." Interestingly enough, here were two Baptist preachers who were light-years apart in their perspectives. Jesse went for the jugular, telling Jerry he sounded like a ventriloquist dummy for Pik Botha.

---

5. When the quadratic equation is solved, one of the factors is the square root of −1. Standard practice is to designate this factor by the sign "i." Mathematical convention is to discard any answers containing this factor. It is real, and it can be squared to equal 1, but it cannot be reduced to any rational sum.

6. Otto, *Idea of the Holy*.

Those who were raised in the church, coming up through the "cradle roll," have heard the text read and interpreted so frequently that there is often little clue concerning where the text ends and theological construction begins. Instruction in the faith is unavoidable, and it is the proper work of every Christian community. However, theologically trained pastors and preachers have the responsibility for examining these constructions so the word can do its sanctifying work. Sometimes it is necessary to prevent the "sins of the fathers" from being passed through the generations. In less serious cases it is necessary to take seriously the inquiring mind and prevent rebellion due to false faith.

An illustration will serve well at this point. I remember being approached by a member who proudly informed me she had purchased a new Scofield bible. My response was polite at best. She insisted that I say more. What I said upset her. I see in retrospect that I may have been excessively brash, but the truth I sought to make was the same. I told her, "I wouldn't give a dime for it." Shocked at the impious response of the pastor, she asked why. My answer was that I prefer my bible and my commentary under separate covers. It had never occurred to her that such a bible teaches a particular theology. She, and others like her, failed to notice the line that separates scripture from the notes that accompany it. The particular theology of Cyrus Scofield, itself derived from John Nelson Darby, is effectively subsumed into the scriptural text.

The same comment may be applied to any system of knowledge in which a set of presuppositions is required to make "correct interpretations." A catechism has its place: let it be what it is. The same principle applies to fundamentalism, scientism, historicism, liberalism, etc. Every critical discourse needs to acknowledge its catechism. The faithful dispenser needs to know these catechisms, whether they are written or oral, whether they are labeled as such or whether they are interwoven with the culture. Identification of catechisms is like the fine art of tuning out static that prevents clear communication. For the preacher, it is like standing in the counsel and knowing the difference between the conflicting noise and the certain sound.

Again, one must be careful in an environment where preaching often seeks to avoid the issues that matter. In such a place, preaching itself often doesn't matter. One can see how that flaw was introduced into American Christianity to soften the church's thousand-year opposition to slavery. Throughout the history of the church there have been debates over the status of servants and slaves within Christian fellowships. On the one hand, the church taught that all who believe on the Lord Jesus are baptized into one body, where there is neither Jew nor Greek, male nor female, slave nor free (Galatians 3:27–28). On the other hand, Christian slaves were taught to obey their masters (1 Timothy 6:1; 1 Peter 2:18). From the Old Testament teaching, a distinction was made between the people of the covenant and the heathens when it came to purchasing slaves (Lev 25:44–46). Manstealing was prohibited, and evangelical demands upon the church required that the gospel be spread to every creature (1 Tim 1:10; Matt 28:19; Mark 16:15. The result was ambiguity and inconsistent teaching in the matter.

In the American churches, abolitionist Christians argued that slavery in every form was inconsistent with the gospel of liberty. The response of slaveholding Christians was to deny that baptism in any way changed one's social status, and to require Christian slaves to disclaim any intention for manumission when seeking admittance to the Table of the Lord.[7]

In defense of bondage, however, the church went further to argue not only a benign or permissive disposition on God's part. The positive argument was made by many to prove that God ordained slavery, cursed the descendants of Ham (the darker races) to be slaves, and regarded as sinful disobedience any acts to be free. Some went so far as to declare that Africans devolve from a separate creation, are beasts and not men, and do not possess souls. Any mixing of the races has its origin in sin, and the quest for social equality is nothing more than an "infidel pestilence."[8]

Again and again, there has been in American Christianity an uncoupling of personal and social holiness, spiritual and secular gospel. Spiritual truth was sectioned off in the regions of the heart, and business was not mixed with ethics and morality. Hence acts could be morally reprehensible, yet legal, and the church refused to speak on matters of justice. Such docetic patterns persist into the present. At the same time, preaching can be obsessed with the spatial coordinates of hell, or what

---

7. See Jones, *African Americans and the Christian Churches 1619–1860*, chapter 1.

8. See Smith, *In His Image, But . . .* , especially chapter 3, "In Defense of Bondage," 129ff.

color robe one wants to wear in heaven. Again, when preaching avoids the issues that matter, the preaching does not matter.

Even when the forms are taken from or suited to the younger, there is content and wisdom that must come from the elder. There can be little dispute that desperate clinging to nineteenth century forms spells the death of the church as we know it. Fewer and fewer from the current generation so much as know the traditions of the fifties, and even smaller numbers desire them. As in the days of Eli, the light in the Tabernacle in Shiloh shows signs of growing dim. Yet it is Eli who knows the voice of God. Even when the call went to Samuel, the old priest was needed to instruct him in saying yes to God. Samuel was vigorous, aggressive, and obedient to God. His works prospered at the hand of God. Wherever he went men trembled in his presence. But he became advanced in years like Eli before him. What's more, his sons were disobedient priests who displeased God, just like the sons of Eli.

For preaching, the methodological question may be restated as a rehearsal of the conversation between God and Rebecca pending the birth of her sons. She wanted to know what was transpiring in her womb that caused such turmoil. The response of the Lord was that there were two nations within her, and the elder would serve the younger. For preaching this is crucial: either the offering will be twenty-first century, or it will be done in solitary. The question is how to preserve the timeless truth of the gospel and present it to a generation so that it can hear it.

This is utterly crucial. Knowing the issues is itself a challenge. In large measure it is how to put critical disciplines in the service of theology. It is ever so easy to grant to analysis more than servant status. Even where it un-conceals the problems and obfuscations, it does not supply the vision for the church. Whether it is Marxism, Rap, or Hip Hop it does not prophesy to set forth the reality that God is creating.

What the preacher is ever seeking is a subject-to-subject encounter in which the hearer meets God. This is the radical language of the Old Testament in the theophanies, where Moses meets God on Sinai, or Isaiah hears the voice of God in the temple. The incarnation of the Son brings a generation face to face with the Son, and in the course of events Phillip is told, "he who has seen me has seen the Father." It is as radical as Saul's encounter on the road to Damascus. It is stated in contemporary parlance in the I-Thou language of Martin Buber.⁹ The image of this encounter is depicted no better than in the instance of the African slave who put the bible to his ear to hear what the ship captain who enslaved him had heard.

And yet, one must test what is heard to know whether it is true. For instance, did the slave and the master hear the same word? It seems they didn't. One heard a word that authorized making slaves of the heathens in perpetuity. The other read from the same chapter (Lev 25) that in the year of Jubilee all who were in bondage were set free. What's more, this is the year that has been declared by the Messiah, upon whom the Spirit has come to rest and in whom the Spirit dwells without measure.

Here the Spirit of wisdom matches the madness and folly of the generation. It exposes it for its true content in pneumatic space where the Spirit performs the work of liberation. One sees this most clearly in the intersection of Christology and pneumatology—preparation of the way for the Son, in the incarnation of the Son, the inauguration of the Son to Messianic office, in the ministry of the Son, and in the sending of the Spirit. The Spirit of liberty turns the hearts of those who believe to the wisdom of the just, prepares a people fit for their God, lifts the poor from the dung heap, and sets free those who are oppressed by the devil (Luke 1:17ff). In other words, where the Spirit of the Lord is, there is liberty.

Preaching with intention opens those spaces through which there can be a pneumatic flow. It plunges the preacher into a spiritual space older exegetes knew as the "sensus plenior." The truth comes forth to embrace—yea, to overwhelm—the one who takes the time and makes preparation to hear. It is an answer to the prayers for the preacher that ask for ". . . his eyes to be set to the telescope of eternity, his ears to be pinned to the wisdom post, for his tongue to be turpentined, and his words turned into sledgehammers of truth."¹⁰ This space is not entered into casually or upon a whim. This ground cannot be traversed without preparation; nor can what is claimed go without testing. Yet this is the surplus given in revelation, without which one is not yet prepared to speak for God.

The work of exegesis serves to modulate the corrupted boundaries in which the hearers dwell. It disturbs the false placidity and undifferentiated ether of a world that has turned from its creator; it punctuates

---

9. Buber, *I and Thou*.
10. Johnson, *God's Trombones*.

the noise of chaos with silences of the Spirit; it charges toxic atmosphere with divine effluvium. Then it translates what has been seen and heard in the counsel of God into auditions that transform ordinary space into a doxological environment wherein God is present. The Lord is in his Holy Temple; let all the earth keep silence. Let the silence be broken only to say, "Speak Lord."

two FROM SCRIBBLE TO SCRIPT:
A SPIRITUALITY OF PREACHING

Preaching comes from the passion of God. God moves graciously toward the creation in an act that is straight from the heart. Like the gift of the Son, God's address is the outflow of love and compassion. In preaching, the unsurpassed gift of God finds its continuation in zeal and work to save the world—to heal the creation and restore it into fellowship. It is addressed to the creature, whose vocation is to lead the creation into obedience to Christ.

As the faithful word of God, preaching has texture fashioned in a life of prayer, discipline, and devotion. Otherwise it is bland, sickening, and obnoxious. It is distasteful to the preacher, and even more so to the people. Few preachers have not had moments when this was their state. Even when people are polite, they are not fed. Only when the preacher draws from the wells of salvation, the deep subterranean streams of the Spirit, is there refreshment for thirsty souls. Deep must call to deep, or there is an act that amounts to forsaking the fountain of living water. Brackish water from broken cisterns is a double iniquity, as the prophet Jeremiah declares with prophetic force.

The script, which begins with scribble, is the instrument of preaching. It is not the sermon; the sermon is what is preached. This instrument may be a written essay; or it may be a set of notes with varying degrees of detail, written or unwritten. Experience and wisdom have dictated to me the prudential value of the essay—as it leaves no question regarding what was intended. Whatever form the script takes, it is an instrument with which the preacher should be comfortable and free. It holds together the tissue and texture, as with a living organism, of the sacrifice that is being offered to God. Accordingly, it is important that the script breathe:

what is inhaled into it during the preparation can be exhaled through the preacher and uttered as a life-giving word to the people of God.

The script that has vitality begins with scribble. In scribble the Spirit is free to brood, hover, inseminate fecundity for the creative work that precedes preaching. It is this pneumatic moment that sets preaching apart from ordinary speech, a lecture, an exercise in rhetoric, or an act of oratory. If preaching is for God, there must be openness for God to infuse it. Otherwise, it remains in a state of "tehom." The fruit remains unripened; the treasures remain buried, as with an egg that does not hatch. Only following incubation is there release of power that permits fruitful speech—speech that performs, that brings forth anything God can call good.

Scribbling here is used as a metaphor to hold together a priceless moment in spirituality wherein meditation and spiritual discipline pass over into an act that is preparatory to speech. The image is that of a pen being moved to touch paper for the sake of capturing what is being received. This moment precedes excessive concern for how communication is to be given, or with what words the utterer will speak. It is the moment at the intersection between the silence from which significant speech emerges and the second in which it may flee. As one grows in the devotion of scribbling, sensitivities to the arts and skills of communication take their place. But first and foremost, scribbling is rooted in the silence from which the living word emerges. It offers those openings through which the divine effluvium can flow; it offers a receptacle the Spirit can penetrate and saturate.

Accordingly, the preacher needs to be in the midst of some life-giving spiritual flow at all times. This may mean following the Daily Office, or some other discipline that carries one into the presence of God. I use the term "carries" with the intention of acknowledging that one's will and determination may be insufficient. Without such discipline it is possible to become so overtaxed with the details and duties of ministry that vital nourishment is neglected. But reading, studying, and preparing to preach are not sufficient. This is not to say that sermon preparation is not a spiritual discipline itself, but rather that a larger, inexhaustible supply is needed for the sustenance of the preacher. The work of preparation can then be taken into the larger life of worship, rather than becoming a chore that is tedious and draining.

Along with regular discipline, the effective preacher does well to remain in some "flow of preaching" at all times. This may mean following a common lectionary, preaching through a book (*lectio continua*), following some modified lectionary, or preaching from a theme to accomplish some purpose in the congregation. Preaching from some flow keeps the preacher from encountering the text as a stranger each week. The text becomes like a subject with whom there is regular interaction and intimacy. Only then does the text speak to yield secrets and knowledge, given to one who can be trusted. From a practical standpoint, one does not have to "re-invent the wheel" each week.

Being prepared to preach requires touching the mystery that is not accessible on the preacher's terms. The mystery of God is given in self-disclosure in moments that are inherent to the mystery. Great risk is involved in presuming to set the time when the mystery can be touched. More time may be required by the mystery than has been allotted. If one makes the approach too late there may not be time to listen, to receive, and to be formed. This is the problem of preaching a draft that stinks, being caught in a bind that affords no alternative. When the mystery has not been touched there is no vitality, no power. Preaching that does not live cannot give life; preaching that has no power cannot give power.

Life-giving preaching springs from a spiritual state that is a place of saturation. This is ether into which one is carried and swept along by the text, and through which the preacher can be carried into the life of the people who hear the word. The instrument of the preacher is the script, but before there is the script, there is the scribble.

Scribble breaks the silence of meditation. One breaks the silence not so much from desire as from necessity. The silence must be broken. The advantage of scribble is that one does not have to have it right: it does not need to be all-together, in order, in shape for observation and critique. Sometimes it is good for the first acts of scribble to be confession of limitation, or the inadequacy one knows in the face of a text. It is amazing what can be taken up into a script to give it traction required to "go somewhere."

Questions about the difficulty of a text may well be included in the scribble. Faithful preachers often wrestle with a word they do not want to declare. Scribble may include a quarrel with God over why a word must be declared, prayer to be sustained for the undertaking. It may even include the rawness of a quarrel with the people. But it is so much better to voice such content in scribble than to let it seep into the script or leak out into the sermon. There is a sense in which scribble offers a moment for the searching and trying of the heart in the presence of God who knows the wickedness of the preacher. It is like prayer in sighs that are too deep for words, but that are suited to one's temperament and mood. Scribble is the extension of meditation in a moment when one can be real with God before standing in the congregation.

This is a moment of "firstness" in which one is confronted by the text as theophany—a burning bush, the word as fire, a boiling cauldron, a plumbline, a basket of figs. This is the midpoint between ineffability and speech. It is at this point that we find the prophet Ezekiel, when he remained speechless for seven days before uttering the oracle. Or, this is the point where the friends of Job appear: they break their silence before having anything worthy to say. False prophets ran before they were sent, and they did not take the time required to stand in the council of God.

Don't be afraid to scribble. Give yourself time to copy what is being inscribed in the spirit by the finger of God. This is the finger that has power to write in a tablet of stone. The finger of God possesses power to cast out devils. It also has power to write a new law in the heart—yea, to inscribe it in the members. Indeed, this is the work the Spirit purposes to do in the preaching of the word.

Tarry, tarry. Take time to scribble, to be moved upon and moved through by inspiration that can stagger the conduit. For some the precious moment will be one in which the scribble will surpass what can be grasped in the reflective state. Some content of preaching can be grasped by the work done with technical precision. Attention must be paid to correctness and the idiom required in order to be understood. But scribble precedes such moments of positive attention. It may well be the case that when the finished product is in hand the scribble will be discarded, but the finished product will be better for having gone through the steps.

Scribble is not to be understood as in opposition to technical work. Often this is what gives rise to the scribble in the first place. It is inclusive of the technical work that supplies the content required for powerful scripting. However, it affords the freedom to begin where one needs to start in the process. Responsible Christian preaching necessarily requires that one preach the word of God. Accordingly, there is a requirement to know what is being said in a discrete pericope. For this knowledge the critical tools are essential. One needs to know the historical setting where possible, what gave rise to the text, the issues being addressed, the genre, the voice, and the audience. For this work commentaries can be extremely helpful—especially in the matter of checking the technical work. However, one must be cautious at the temptation to go to the commentary of another too soon, especially when the hermeneutical judgments and decisions of another interfere with the vitality of the word. The method of many commentators is to ascertain what can be known about a text without relying on the claims concerning God.

Christian scripture is to be interpreted within the community of faith. This includes the great cloud of witnesses, which encompasses those who had faith before this era. While contemporary commentary can assist in identifying errors and underdevelopment in scientific and historical knowledge, they are not necessarily superior when it comes to theological insight and sensitivity to revelation. There is a real sense in which what we now call historical and systematic theology is the effort of the church throughout the ages to read the scriptures correctly. Hence these disciplines must also be appropriated to avoid the "private interpretation" of one generation and muting interlocutors from the ages.

Dogmatic theology has its place. It sets a perimeter around the speech that may be uttered by Christians. It forces every discourse to be consistent with beliefs that put one within or outside the boundary of truth. The creeds of the church are quite convenient in this regard. But they should be accompanied by knowledge of what they eliminate along with the confession. Dogmatics aids us in avoiding speaking errors, even when the intent is to simplify. Systematic theology is essential for insuring that whatever is said in one matter is consistent with what else must be said. In addition, it assists one in speaking in a way that is coherent with other knowledges, supplying a critique of them where necessary.

Christian preaching must not neglect to speak to the world. This is the prophetic task that discloses the subjectivity of those who hear the gospel. It exposes the wisdom of this world and casts down the false knowledge that opposes the gospel. In this regard the modern preacher must do like the ancient preacher Koheleth, who gave his mind to know madness and folly. Here knowledge of the social sciences is crucial: it offers indispensable tools for analysis. The same is so of science. But these knowledges must also be known at their presuppositional level so that they remain servants of the preacher rather than his or her master. For what we preach is Christ.

Attention is paid to the time of the liturgical year and the calendar—to holy days and holidays. The same is so of issues within the world, the nation, and the community being addressed. While it is not given for us to know the times and seasons reserved to the Father's power, it is for us to know the times and seasons in which we preach. These data are to be taken to the text, to see what the Lord has to say in the matter through the text that has been given. In seeking to hear from God through the text rather than hunting for a text that "fits the occasion," unanticipated beams of heaven guide our footsteps in this wilderness below.

Scribble enables one to bring to the task all the content required for scripting as a spiritual exercise. It is sort of like making a cake: all the ingredients need to be at one's fingertips before the process of mixing batter begins. How horrible to be in the midst of mixing batter, only to discover that one has no eggs! True, you may have more than is needed for a specific preparation, but it is better to have more than is needed than to find yourself without the crucial ingredient. Surely the time will come for making another cake.

Between scribbling and scripting, close and scrupulous attention is needed to the audience. That is, explicit attention is needed to the "world in front of the text." Matters such as how a congregation hears are utterly important. This requires knowledge of the times, the cultures, the stimuli that operate, the level of knowledge, the images that resonate within the hearers. The preacher dare not ignore questions such as whether content is better grasped by a linear, logical presentation, or whether the cluster of images is more effective. Gaps and breaks in knowledge as one goes from one generation to another are likewise significant. If we speak of the Bay of Pigs, a sizeable portion of adults in many congregations will be lost. What triggers knowledge, and what associations enable comprehension, are highly relevant issues.

Accordingly, between the scribble and the script careful attention must be given to order and flow. In some cases it may be advantageous to include some "scheme of recovery" in the scribble. One must be mindful of what must be said to be correct, and how it must be said to be heard. It is good to spend at least one sitting with the scribble for the purpose of imposing order and arrangement on the content. I am reminded here of the early days of computer programming, where students were required to produce a flow chart to show all the operations.

A few minds are nimble enough to do this in the head. Most of us will need some sort of code, something on the order of the "merge feature" on computers, or an old fashioned outline to insure the right flow from the perspective of the hearer. Such is the challenge of causing persons to see with their ears. What is achieved is "synethesia"—a unity of the senses, where the word speaks to the entire person. We do not preach to brains, intellects, or emotions, but to persons. The aim of preaching is to cause persons to see what we have been shown in the council of God. But what we have been given is words, and when the Spirit breathes through them the word of God is heard. This is a word that opens eyes and causes hearts to burn.

Scripting portends a spiritual space that one enters for the purpose of preparing what has been received as a gift from God to the people. One must make preparation to enter that space, as it cannot be gainsaid. What one has from scribble can be juxtaposed in such a manner that it opens this discursive space. Like mixing batter, the ingredients interpenetrate and interact with one another. Sugar and flour are in the cake, but they do not stand out as separate ingredients. The same is so with exegesis and analysis: they may blend in such a manner that when one speaks the words of the text the application to the congregation is apparent. Such a pattern is a mark of good preparation. The word buried in a specific text can speak to a given moment. An angle of vision not arrived at by chance can be achieved.

When preparation has been made well, scripting can be on the order of an "ecstatic moment" in which one steps outside her self and into her office (practice) as preacher. Here one finds words and phrases that are gifts. Illustrations make the gospel perspicuous. Images declare far more content than one was capable of understanding. The mystery touched, the preacher becomes the mouthpiece—the oracle of God, a flute through which the divine breath is blown. A preacher has cheated herself and her congregation if she has not reached this moment when she becomes the instrument of the Spirit's scripting.

The technical work insures against errors, even when wings are given to the spirit. Even in the state of ecstasy, one is not permitted to speak errors. Indeed, because God is faithful and cannot deny himself, the Spirit who leads into truth sensitizes against untruth. The technical work is something like one parallel rail on a set of train tracks: without both rails the train is wrecked.

This spiritual space allows one to enter into something of a mystical moment that can be compared to Taborian Light and a state of tranquility (*hesychasm*—to use the language of the East). This is where the work of scripting passes over into worship. This is a moment in which the pen glides over the page, or the fingers dance over the keyboard. The right word comes. The work is worship. Preparation can be as rewarding as delivery—which in some instances is anticlimactic.

This is the overflow seen in the call of Moses, who stood before the bush that burned without being consumed and received the commission from God. The ministry of Ezekiel is marked indelibly by the moment when he fell on his face as the vision was received and the word was inserted into his mouth. Throughout their labors, the disciples referred to the events of Tabor, when the light irradiated the Lord, and Moses and Elijah appeared while the voice spoke to proclaim him as the Son. On the Isle of Patmos John heard the voice like waters and saw in a vision the Risen Christ.

No gift to the preacher is greater than being moved to write and speak from a silence that is spiritual plentitude. This is silence before God that is everything but empty. It is a silence into which one carries all the labors they are capable of bringing, and it is filled by the presence of God. The silence is full and not empty. It is not the silence of one who has nothing to say; it is the silence of one who waits to know what must be said. It is a pregnant silence from which comes the speech that is the necessity of the moment.

This speech is the overflow of spiritual discipline: prayer, meditation, study, and reading. It is an investment in the ministry of the word where the preacher is the conduit. This is a gracious space, for one who knows he does not have sufficient words lives with confidence that the reservoir does not run dry. Time and time again, the source is replenished even as it flows.

The Risen Christ presents the living word and breathes out the Spirit, making use of the preacher as instrument. It is an act of worship done to the glory of God the Father who dwells in light inaccessible. The offering is like a sweet smelling savor, and the one who makes the offering is blessed by the fragrance.

Since preaching is an art form that relies on an extensive set of skills, the preacher must remain in search for methods and techniques to best accomplish the task. But more than all else, preparing to preach requires openness to the living word through which the Risen Christ, who breathes the Spirit into the church, speaks to the church.

three NUTS AND BOLTS:

A HOW-TO GUIDE FOR PREACHERS

Numerous books on the subject of preaching are available. In most cases, that is what they are indeed—i.e., books *about* preaching. Some of the classic texts that deal with "how to" are John A. Broadus, H. Grady Davis, and James Earl Massey. They were supplanted by a more general sort of text that looked at preaching as a more narrative form, or that were less pronounced regarding how the sermon "fits and holds" together—Long, Craddock, Buttrick. Then there are the specialized texts like Mitchell, LaRue, and Tisdale, and Harris, Lowry, Wilson, Stookey, etc.[1]

While it is true that preaching is far more than "technique," there is value in giving some attention to "how to." My approach to this work grows largely out of the matrix of one deeply invested in the practice of preaching on a regular basis. Not only do I teach it: I do it. Then I reflect on it as one who is trained theologically. Even more, I have the clear sense of "doing theology" with every sermon preparation.

In both preaching and teaching preaching, one gets into the "marrow of the work" in the course of doing it. There must be a beginning point, which may come with either the technical or the artistic. The object is to "gain access" to the discursive space and enter the terrain where the content flows. One disposition passes over into the other. There is an "umbilical exchange" in this "pneumatic flow" as the tissue of the text clings to the ligaments' structure and design. Nevertheless, it is worth stepping back to examine the building blocks of a sermon.

---

1. Broadus, *On Preparation and Delivery*; Davis, *Design for Preaching*; Massey, *Designing the Sermon*; T. G. Long, *Witness of Preaching*; Mitchell, *Black Preaching*; Craddock, *Preaching*; Buttrick, *Homiletic*; LaRue, *Heart of Black Preaching*; Lowry, *Homiletical Plot*; Harris, *Word Made Plain*; Stookey, *Calendar: Christ's Time for the Church*; Tisdale, *Preaching as Local Theology and Folk Art*.

Building Blocks for the Sermon

Nothing is more frustrating in attempting to craft the sermon than attempting to write without having something to say. One does not have something to say worth listening to as preaching simply for choosing a text, or for merely feeling deeply and passionately about some issues. There is work that must be done: intense work, spade work, unrelenting work.

In this sense, one should regard the sermon as a creative work. The ingredients must be set in place—all that is needed for the production. Like making bread, creating a sculpture, etc., one gets everything in place, and then they begin to work. This is the work of mixing, blending, with intention and proportion. Or, one can make the comparison to building a house: before the work gets started there must be the assembling of the supplies.

Building blocks set before the preacher the content with which the work is to be done. Only then can there be appropriate judgments of inclusion, elimination, sequence and flow, so there can be intelligibility in the work of preaching. The term "blocks" is being used, but it is really more like "material" that interacts and interpenetrates. That would be "blocks" more in the sense of bricks or stones fastened together with mortar that sets up and becomes nearly as hard as the rock. Or it may be blocks in the sense of the "living stones" that comprise the temple as habitation of God. Without the life of one stone passing on and receiving life from the other there is no temple with vitality and endurance.

Another value of the concept of the "blocks" is the simple fact that in more cases than not the sermon is more than one can conceive as a whole. Even when one does have the image or picture in their mind, it is all but impossible to wrap the mind around every detail. Even more, one must be prepared to test the "impressions" that are received about a text in moments of pondering, meditation, and openness to revelation. Even when the claim for revelation is divine inspiration, there remains the need for testing. By this means, one can "prove all things," and "hold fast to what is good."

As intelligible communication, however, this matter of design is essential. No matter how clear and potent a sermon may be in the mind of the preacher, it means little or nothing to the hearer if there is no clarity, no sequence, no order, no coherence. Indeed, there must be some degree of anticipation of how the worshipping congregation hears and processes knowledge. One cannot disregard the hearer—the congregation—in preaching that is worth the time it takes to deliver.

BLOCK ONE: EXEGESIS

Dare I say it; dare you believe it? The heart and soul of Christian preaching is exegesis. This is the work that "brings out" what is given in the text. Another way of putting the matter is that, as preachers, we have no more to give than what has been given to us. In this regard, the meal of Jesus with the disciples at the Table is the mark of Christian ministry. He broke the bread, and gave it to them. They (we) are to give to the entire world the life in God that has been extended to us. The first move is to "bring out" what has been given in the world.

There is no shortage of texts on this matter of exegesis. Every preacher "and his mammy" has heard the plea for faithfulness to the text. Exegesis is "bringing out," rather than "reading in" to a text. Numerous texts explore in detail this crucial work, providing essential tools, rich insight, and valuable techniques.[2]

Two critical comments can be made of exegesis: 1) It requires an excursion into all knowledges that are essential for bringing out meaning; and 2) In its broader scope this includes all that is pertinent for constructing a text, including the manifold traditions of the church and those traditions that might be regarded as misinterpretation.

One of the best illustrations of what is entailed in this "excursion" is reading the headlines of a newspaper and contemplating the knowledges required to make sense of it. Say for instance that the headlines concerning the World Cup in Soccer, or the budget crisis of a small HBCU (Historically Black College or University) were being discussed. Imagine such a paper being read by a person two thousand years ago. Or even imagine a person two thousand years from now reading that paper.

With soccer, for instance, an account would be needed of this game that is called football on the world scene, as compared to what is called

---

2. One of the best summaries in this regard is an article by Richard Hays in the Willimon and Lischer volume, *Concise Enclyclodedia of Preaching*. See Hays, "Exegesis." Another helpful summary text is Soulen and Soulen, *Handbook of Biblical Criticism*.

football in countries like the United States and Canada. Some sense would need to be made of the rules, the conditions, and the strategies employed to gain victories. Why, for instance, in one game, is there so much involvement with the feet, while in another game there is so much use of the hands?

With an HBCU: what is the nature of the parallel institutions along lines of race. Indeed, even the concept of race may well need to be made explicit, given the other measures by which humans have classified themselves in the long sweep of human history. There is a "race history" peculiar to the United States that is not duplicated in other countries of the world. Because it makes sense only in that setting, a thorough knowledge of the history would be essential for making sense of the headline and the accompanying story. Other knowledges essential for the task of preaching will be discussed below, however the reason they are mentioned here (even if only obliquely) is to challenge the notion early on that the necessary preparatory work for preaching has been completed when one has read the commentaries.

Christian preaching is from the bible, the written word of God. Debates come and go concerning how this sacred text is to be read. Some of the best insight comes from what the scriptures have to say of themselves. Mind you, what the scriptures say of themselves is radically different from what is said in philosophical or hard scientific approaches to the biblical text. One of the clearest scriptural statements in this regard is from 2 Timothy: "All scripture is given by inspiration of God, and is profitable for doctrine, for reproof, for correction . . . that the man [woman] of God may be perfect, thoroughly furnished unto all good works" (2 Tim 3:16–17). This passage, often taken wrongly as a proof-text for Fundamentalism, goes a long way in saying what the proper disposition to scripture should be. This text contains no claim for scripture being error-free in matters of science and history—hardly a concern in the first century as it is in our day. Rather the concern seems to be more for the meaning and performance of scripture as the living word of God.

Put another way, holy scripture is "God-breathed." It has its origin in the very life of God. It goes forth, like the Spirit, to give life and vitality (see reflections of this perspective on the scriptures in the marvelous tribute to the law in Ps 19). To use the picturesque exegesis of slave-preaching, "the sun hitches up his ponies early in the morning to make his trek across the sky."³ The law of the Lord is perfect, converting the soul.

Or again, there is the wonderful claim concerning the scriptures from the epistle that bears the name of the apostle Peter. He insists that the scriptures result from holy men of old being moved by the Spirit. Of course, the same Spirit who supplies the writing is vigilant over his word to perform it. The interpretation of scripture is not to be a private affair. Rather, any word spoken by prophetic utterance is subject to be measured by the test of others within the believing and worshipping community.

When preaching from a passage of scripture one of the first issues to be raised has to do with the "book" from which a lection is taken. Located as we are within the Christian Era, there are often unfounded positive assumptions regarding the bible. Not only is the setting of the limits on the canon an historic act of the church; there are other writings that have necessarily been excluded. Those that are included are present with a purpose. One of the first questions to be raised by an exegete is why a given book was written. Then one wants to know why it was preserved, why it has been included in the canon, and why it is inserted in the location where it is found.

For the most part, the "books" were separate scrolls (with the exception of the Torah, called the five books of Moses). These scrolls were self-contained, and they could be read separately (if not independently) of one another. Invariably, there was some occasion for their writing. There is some interest(s) being addressed in the text. Something of consequence is at stake. In short, the book was written because something mattered. So here we come to the first question of good exegesis—namely, the "So What?" of the text. Why, for instance, would anyone sit to write the first book of the bible—Genesis, the book of beginnings? Clearly, the writer was not present for firsthand observation of what is given in the account.

---

3. In a famous sermon, "The Sun Do Move," preacher and former slave John Jasper debates from the pulpit with those who had taken a strictly scientific approach to the text of scripture. He describes the sun as a subject obedient to divine commands, and draws a parallel between the law and the sun, referring specifically to Psalm 19:5–6. The sun is described by the psalmist as dwelling in a tabernacle, from which it goes forth like a strong man to run a race, with the circuit being from one end of the heavens to the other. For Jasper's sermon, see LaRue, *Heart of Black Preaching*, 132.

With the New Testament writings the reason and purpose are often much clearer. In the Lucan corpus, the reason is given explicitly at the beginning of both parts (the Gospel of Luke and the Acts of the Apostles). In the fourth gospel, the reason is stated at the end of chapter 20. And with many of the epistles, the reason is given in the very name of the epistle. Either they are written to a specific church, or they are written as letters to be circulated among the churches stated in the salutation. With most books of the Old Testament, no such clarity is present. One must read the book carefully, paying attention to the setting, along with other items of political, social, and economic interest.

Inasmuch as the interest of these writers was knowledge of God's will and work among the people, they must be called theologians. Their perspective is crucial for comprehending the way they interpreted their data. In some instances such judgment is a crucial factor in what they so much as consider. Additionally, one can find points of tension and debate between one writer and another. For instance, in Job there is a clear and open quarrel with the Deuteronomistic view, which says that blessing is the sign of divine approbation and suffering is the sign of punishment for wrongdoing. Job, the central character, calls on God for his witness that he is a righteous man. Note that this is precisely the word God has for the adversary at the outset of the book.

It is good for a preacher to have a working knowledge of any book from which she intends to preach. Indeed, it is advisable for every preacher to develop a working knowledge of each book within the canon as a basic set of tools used in the work of exegesis.

Exegesis is improved greatly when one can look at biblical texts as "living words." What is meant here is not that the words were divinely dictated. Rather, the written word is inspired. To use the language of Peter, those who wrote were "moved by the Holy Ghost." They sought and grasped the meaning of living under God within the community of the covenant. But more, they discussed these matters openly and candidly with others involved in the same quest. When one reads without the superimposition of an extraneous theory that requires consensus of opinion, this motif is clear. Similarly, if one does not require a unity of focus that has eluded even modern students and scholars, one can actually appreciate the candor with which the mystery of God is pondered.

The various approaches to the mystery may be compared with the various sketches required for the reproduction of the architect's view of the building to be constructed. The top view can show only one perspective. The same must be said for each elevation that is shown. Even the composite must be skewed in order to show depth. Taken together, these views render an offering that communicates to those who carry out the construction the knowledge required for them to proceed.

Attention must be paid to the location of texts. The assumption operating at this point is that location is not done at random. One can see from the Old Testament how the books are grouped. The same is so for the books of the New Testament. With the first five books of the Old Testament, or the first four books of the New Testament, for instance, there is some value in reading them in series—as if one builds upon the other. But a dogged insistence that they ought to be read in this manner limits severely what can be gleaned. Far more valuable insight comes from searching out and finding what the perspective really was. For instance, while Exodus, Numbers, and Deuteronomy cover the same time frame and much of the same content, one can see upon closer inspection that the projects vary significantly.

Where possible it is good to know the source of texts. However, it is equally important to know how a text lays claim to its authority. In some instances writings bear the name of the author. In other instances no name is given at all. There are also writings that bear the name of some worthy or revered person whose authorship is questionable at best when canons of modern historiography are applied. Yet the name adds clarity for reflecting upon the times in question; the attribution lends cogency to the issues under consideration and supplies gravity for the authority being claimed. In Old Testament writings authenticity was associated with heroes like Moses, Joshua, Samuel, and David. In the New Testament authority flowed from the persons who had been with Jesus and numbered among the apostles.

Good exegesis cannot happen without regard for a text's genre. It makes a difference whether a piece of writing is a poem, a song, or a prayer. The same is also true for what is claimed as an act of God. There is no concern with proving that the event occurred for one who was the witness. Indeed, it is not even necessary to believe what is seen. The seeing itself is sufficient. The meaning can be missed entirely if we do not properly note the genre. A song of praise is about the mighty work of God. It is not a statement of science, or a claim about what is "possible." Or, to use the language of Gabriel in response to Mary's question about possibility: "with God nothing shall be impossible" (Luke 1:37). More than all else, sacred writ is a story about God's gracious dealings. First it is with the people of God's choice; then it is a story of the blessing that God bestows upon all creation. From among all the families of the earth, God chose a people for the praise of his glory.

Within both the Old and New Testaments, there are summaries of this story. One such summary is what the children were required to recite when they came to present their gifts and offerings to the Lord. It began with the wandering Aramean, Abram, who went down into the land of Egypt. There, God made him a great and prosperous nation. Another is in the apostolic preaching of the New Testament. There, a thread is woven through the history of the Hebrews, and it is folded into the lineage of David, the king from whom the Messiah was to descend, as one can see clearly in Acts 2 and 7.

One might go so far as to say that the choice of God created history. This is the sense in which the prophetic perspective is inserted. For the most part, history is the chronicle of the mighty and powerful. It is about the succession of kings, their sons, and sometimes their wives and daughters. Essentially history is about who sits on the throne, and who has the power to dethrone him. One can see even from the hand of the Chronicler an attempt to "tidy-up" David, the man after God's own heart. As a matter of fact, when one gets in the sawdust trail of David, as he is "tidied up" by the Chronicler, one almost wonders whether the same person is being brought into view.

In addition to the flow of the story, the particular words that authors chose to use are also important. There is no substitute for being able to read the text in the language in which it was written. Then one can see nuances, shades of meaning, and tone of conversation. This is what lets one in on the action that gives the text the quality of being the living word. Much of the meaning and action are locked into words. Word study grants access to the thought-world of the writer. The etymology, the descriptive quality, the deposit of meaning found in a word cannot be replaced in any other way. Often it is the precise word, with its shade of meaning, that unlocks the text or that gives the clue for how it is to be constructed.

Because of the distance to be covered by time, history, culture, etc., the text is not self-interpreting. It is true: even the act of selecting and reading scripture is interpretation. The question is not whether one interprets; the question is whether the work of interpretation is done well or done poorly.

Another passage that often gets messed up in this regard has to do with a word about scripture that is found in the scriptures themselves. That is, "no prophecy of scripture is of private interpretation" (2 Pet 1:20–21). Contrary to the meaning set forth by radical literalists, this is a passage that calls for communal interpretation. In this case it would have been the bishop charged with oversight of the churches, or the council in which bishops met for the defense of the faith.

In other words, the work of interpretation is not to be done privately. Rather, there is to be a community of interpretation. The assumption here is that the Spirit who inspired the word gives illumination. That illumination is not all a matter of private preference. There does come the point at which teaching is dangerous to the Church. Recall the scene of the Ethiopian eunuch in the travel to which Phillip joins himself. The summary of the conversation was that the eunuch, no matter who he was in the cabinet, could not be expected to come up with "the sense and understanding" on his own (Acts 8).

There need be no great anxiety over the fact of difference of opinion in the interpretation of texts. The history of the church is lined with contests of this sort. Indeed, one might say that the rise of creeds and dogmas was an attempt to discourage private interpretation of the sort that leads to denial of the faith. Remember, heretics were some of the most pious persons to be found. As they saw the matter, they were following the logic of what was given by setting it against the grid of their own logic.

Block Two: Thesis

The thesis is what makes the sermon stand up and go somewhere. Without it the sermon lies like a jellyfish—limp, lifeless. It goes nowhere. Indeed the thesis is what distinguishes the sermon from a mere exhortation, testimony, account of one's experience.

A great teacher of preaching who had much to say regarding the thesis is Miles Jones.[4] The thesis is bound inextricably for him with what it means to preach. With the thesis something is wagered, something is advanced. It is not a statement of what is obvious. It is not a statement without any consequence. The thesis is what makes the argument worth advancing. The thesis is consequential, for instance, as is the case with the proclamation that Jesus is Lord.

The thesis states forthrightly the specific proclamation of the sermon being preached. It advances what is of consequence in a given pericope in a tensional matter that forces a statement of rebuttal or further explanation. The thesis is what disallows indifference. In its face one cannot say glibly, "so what?" It is like the confrontation between the prophet and the people on Mount Carmel. They are pressed to choose whom they will serve. If God is God, they are compelled to serve him. On the other hand, if Baal is god, they must serve him. The consequence is ever-present. For whomever is their god, that one they will serve.

Or again, for the early church: either Jesus is the Christ, the Son of the living God, or he is just another in a series of prophets. The confession and proclamation of the deity and lordship of Jesus left no room for indifference. To confess him would result in them being put out of the synagogue. It forced a separation with fellow Jews who could not so confess. It forced confrontation and separation from Greeks to whom this gospel was foolishness.

The thesis makes all the difference in the sermon. It serves like a spine to distribute the content throughout the sermon. It prevents content from "hanging off" the sermon, like clothes that won't fit. It is the principle factor that counters incoherence. By means of it there can be some "testing of the content" to see whether it fits the given sermon, or whether it should be reserved for another time.

The thesis may well be the most difficult part of writing in a given sermon. Often it cannot be written until after the sermon has been drafted. For this reason one may not be well advised to wait on their thesis before getting to work. Very often it grows out of the struggle for clarity. Indeed, there is a sense in which one needs to know what they have a hold of before trying to make essential connections.

---

4. Jones's unpublished works can be found on tapes in the library of the Samuel Dewitt Proctor School of Religion, Virginia Union University, Richmond, Virginia.

The thesis is particularly important for the sermon that has more than one move, or that is more than the mere telling of the story. It anticipates the moves and shows how the content is crucial for the preaching of a given text.

Block Three: Theological Issues

From the outset it is crucial to understand, and even more crucial to state, that preaching is a theological task. It cannot be otherwise. So much as making a comment about the acts of God involves a theological move. Any account of an experience, any report of a divine deed, thrusts one into the work of thinking about God. Any act that disclaims the theological task for preaching should be shunned like the plague.

First and foremost, the texts that we preach are claims about God. One might ascertain some history in them, and one may need to know even more history to interpret them, but first and foremost, they are about God. The subject is God, the primary actor is God. The first word we get is a testimony to God—"In the beginning, God"; the last word is God—"Even so, come Lord Jesus" (Gen 1:1, Rev 22:20). Even when human actors are permitted on the scene, it is about God.

Critical study of the scriptures either states the theological presuppositions involved in the work, or it intends to set theological claims and suppositions aside to do the work. Either position is theological. Actually, what is called exegetical or "biblical" studies at present was formerly enfolded into the larger work of preaching and teaching the faith. It is only within the last few hundred years that there has been an effort of any sort to divide the disciplines, and set aside theology as separate from the rest. Put another way, all the work that is done in preparing to preach is theology, even when other knowledges are made servants to the task.

It is not possible to overstate the significance of reading the scriptures within a "community of interpreters." The reading and interpreting of the scriptures is not to be a matter of private interpretation. Similarly, it is the utmost arrogance to assume that modern generations are the only ones with anything of value to say concerning the meaning of the scriptures.

The concern here is not to downplay the significance of critical study. Rather, it is to insist that this too is theological work. The modern exegete is no less theological than Clement, Origen, Chrystosom, Augustine, Calvin, or Luther. Ironically, some are even more theological by their disclaimers. It is important in this regard to cite the work of David Steinmetz on pre-critical readings of the texts. One might also want to look at the work of John Dominic Crossan in this regard as well.

The first move in preparing a sermon ought not be going to the commentary; yet, that move should not be neglected. It is important to hear from God first—to hear what the Spirit has to say to the church through a particular passage of scripture, on a particular day, to a particular collection of worshipping people. And yet, there can be great value in hearing what another has seen and heard.

Interpreters from throughout the ages should be considered companions, a company of believers, a cloud of witnesses. They are essential for testing "impressions" received from a text. Revelation often has a partial and fragmentary shape. No harm can be done by seeing what another has to say in the matter.

Attention needs to be given to "misinterpretation" as well. The intention may have been good when the books of heretics were burned. However, it can be argued that one of the best ways to "keep the way clear" is to know what is littering the pathway. The history of heresy is essentially a chronicle of misinterpretation. Heretics were denounced as impious; many were killed as the quintessence of evil and contamination. But in more cases than not, they were giving their "private interpretations" to matters that needed to be settled in the larger council of those who had been made "wise unto salvation." The "right division" of the scriptures and adequate reasoning about God need the counsel of many who have given their lives to this work.

Crass and crude misinterpretation of texts within the larger tradition of the church must not be set aside, even if such interpretations are regarded as primitive. The truth of the matter is that some of the most primitive teaching to be found is actually the most modern. This is especially true when such errors are not known, so they can serve to mark boundaries and act as guideposts. In this regard, great service is supplied by hermeneutical theologies, such as black theology, liberation theology, feminist and womanist theology.

Again and again, the point of departure for these theologies is a misreading of texts, or constructions of texts that have been read back into them. It is the work of theology to make clear where the reading of scripture ends and the construction of the text begins. This is where the work of theology is undertaken, whether with intention or by default.

Issues that reach the status of doctrine or dogma lie along a locus (a path, a boundary) of issues that matter. Again, it is nothing short of cultural arrogance to denigrate the issues of previous generations as if they were mere nitpicking persons absorbed with what is trivial. We have no way of knowing what the verdict will be in generations to come for the issues we prioritize, or even for those we neglect or relegate to insignificance.

One of the great banes of the American church has been to disengage its theology from what matters in the life of the people. One of the earliest traces of this dangerous theological isotope was the opinion by the bishop of London. In an effort to assuage the fear of slaveholders—that making Christians of their slaves would turn them into their equals—he stated that "baptism and admission to the Table of the Lord do not affect one's standing"[5] Neither does it change the relationship of one Christian to another. For centuries it had been the wisdom of the church that fellow Christians do not hold one another in bondage, and baptism had been the occasion for the release of the former slave. Bound to Christ, there was no other master to whom one was required to do obeisance.

This pattern of disengagement, which I prefer to call "American Docetism," remains alive and well in the American church—in both hemispheres. Alongside this tendency is an emergent pattern among the "wretched of the earth" to read the bible among themselves. What is discovered is the amazing affinity between the words of the scriptures and the needs of those who suffer political and economic oppression. And that word is far more than "slaves obey your masters," or that honest service redounds to greater rewards in heaven.

The preacher can ill afford to disregard or treat lightly the dogmatic positions taken by the church. It cannot be stated with too much frequency or force that the issues were not ripped out of thin air. They belong in a constellation of issues that matter deeply. They grow out of an effort to interpret the scriptures and to guard the flock over which the shepherds have been made overseers.

---

5. Sernett, *African-American Religious History*.

Dogmatic issues indicate the confessions and mysteries concerning which there is to be no debate. As the writer of Timothy puts the matter, the mystery of godliness is without controversy (1 Tim 3:16). The good confessions are given. They are not given so much to understand as to be confessed. They mark the boundaries that put one within or without the faith. And in preaching, as much as if not more than any other endeavor, we "contend earnestly" for this faith. It has already been delivered unto the saints.

The critical outline of dogma is found within the creeds of the church. Even those who claim not to have creeds do well to familiarize themselves with these thresholds and boundaries in matters of faith. To do less is to forfeit the wisdom of many. Even when one cannot use the identical language within their "tradition," they do well to know it. Even more, it is important to know the issues. Here is where the critical task of theology is so significant: accounting for what matters in a doctrine of the church gives clues for what matters in preaching. Preaching that does not take up what matters is not relevant: it does not matter.

As preacher it is crucial to know when one has walked upon a "lode" in the text. It is to be mined, and not undermined. It is not to be treated as irrelevant, minute detail, or obsession with argument for the sake of itself. It is more like the irritating grain of sand that gives rise to the beautiful pearl, or the tiny piece of carbon that over the years crystallizes into the most beautiful diamond.

Issues that give rise to the specific and larger traditions of the church should be acknowledged in preaching. The faithful dispenser of the word needs to know what unfaithful dispensation is. Knowledge of unfaithful dispensation serves as a monitor for the preacher and enables faithful warning for the people. This does not require that one turn the pulpit into a place for brawling, but it does call for constructions of texts in the act of preaching that fortify the people.

One is not well prepared to preach if they do not know the long, rich, deep, and contested dogmatic traditions of the church. But neither is one well prepared if they know how to preach only within the narrow confines of their local tradition. Or, to put the matter another way, the criteria being discussed at present cohere with standards by which one should exhort according to the grace and inspiration that is given, as distinct from the one who is "ordained" to be a teacher of the faith. It was not for naught that the apostle admonished that not many should be masters, or that the apostle urged those who would listen to wait on ministries that require right division of the word.

When the church marched with the powers of the magistrate and the sword it was reasonable to speak emphatically regarding what the church has to say in the matter. But in our day the segmentation of the church into denominations is real, and cannot readily be set aside. Even the "non-denominations" operate as denominations. On occasion it is almost tempting to refer to the "nondenominational denomination." It looks, swims, and quacks like a duck. There will therefore be precious little sympathy for insisting that it is a dog. In short, one must have functional knowledge of the "ersatz dogmas" operating within denominational and local churches that never reach the form of creeds or encyclicals. Yet they have either "life-giving" or "deadly" powers.

While dogmatics gives attention to the good confession that has been made and delivered to the saints, systematics gives attention to the knowledges that compete for the mind and obedience of the subject of preaching. It encompasses the wisdom of the age.

On the one hand, systematics can be apologetic, showing how faith in Jesus as Lord and Christ is reasonable. We see the tendency in this direction in some of the Pauline teaching. For instance, in Acts 17 where Paul preaches to the Athenians. Again, we see this motif in the early church where further attempts are made at correlating the gospel of Jesus Christ to the systems of knowledge that were prevalent in the world.

A problem arises with systematics if the center, the anchor, the grounding is lost. Then it becomes essentially an answering enterprise. Implicit in the flawed approach is that the world knows the questions to ask, and that the knowledges that "exalt themselves" against the gospel really have the right to do the interrogating. We see the germ of this problem for the modern church with Schleiermacher, who pitched his work to the "despisers" of the faith. We see it again with Tillich, for whom Christianity was essentially an "answering" religion.

Without systematics one can easily take the position that capitulates to the knowledges of science and history, granting them center stage. This produces a whole set of problems. We have already acknowledged the potential for turning the faith into an "answering machine." Another potential problem is that theology loses its critical capacity to speak to the world. Still another is the act of capitulation that seeks to reformat the content of the faith to correspond to the epistemology of science and history. Then the living word is reduced truly to a dead letter.

Systematics is necessary for confronting the hearer of the gospel with his or her own subjectivity. This is as important in the "enlightened West" as in the so-called primitive cultures. Here is how one makes the decision regarding culture. One approach is to regard culture as "preparatory" to the hearing of the gospel. Then one finds the "proto-evangelical" strains so that knowledge can be "baptized" in the service of the gospel. One can see this pattern clearly as oriental culture is appropriated through Moses and subsequent students and teachers of the law in Ancient Israel. It is seen again—and, perhaps, with greater clarity—in the confrontation between the gospel and Hellenistic thought.

The church fathers were particular with showing where the lines of demarcation stood. Even when the concepts were Hellenistic, there was insistence that the content be measured by the mystery of the gospel. Many attempts to make the gospel more palatable were rejected in the early church. Indeed, one might say this is the very root of the problem with heresy—namely, terminology and thought forms with pre-existing meaning in cultures around the realm of the Mediterranean were not subjected to an adequate theological test. That matter has not diminished through the ages.

Systematics further interrogates the knowledges of the culture. It is reminiscent (methodologically speaking) of the banter that took place between Paul and the philosophers he encountered. On one occasion he called for them, saying, "where is the wise man . . . the sage . . . the debater." He went on to say that "since the world through wisdom was not saved, it has pleased God through the foolishness of preaching to save them that believe" (1 Cor 1:21).

Systematics can and does go to the very presuppositions of knowledge. It exposes what Michael Polanyi called the "tacit dimension."[6] This is knowledge that is assumed by virtue of being immersed within a culture. This knowledge disguises itself, with the worst stunt of all being the pretense that it does not exist, or that it is simply given with the world.

With what knowledge do we begin a day? And on what knowledges must one rely? The tendency with most of us is to take a positive view to-

---

6. Polanyi, *Tacit Dimension*.

ward the world. That is, we assume the knowledges we need to negotiate a day as if they are given with the world. The number of those who know the foundation in physics for electricity, magnetism, or friction is low. Indeed, with the decreasing emphasis on theoretical knowledge the tide of positivism rises, and it is increased exponentially with the proliferation of technology.

The consequences for preaching are enormous. The subject constituted in a frame of reality founded upon technology scarcely comes to terms with the boundaries: sickness, natural disaster, and death are exceptions in this regard. For the most part life is lived as if under the control of the subject, and the positive knowledges supply both explanation and means for domination.

To put the matter another way, technology supplies a pantheon of lesser deities to replace the imminent God of theistic faith. At best, God is a deistic cipher, who sets the world in motion, who is summoned when the lesser deities prove inadequate, or who is to be supplicated when the acts are considered a disaster.

It makes sense, then, that there would be increasing incompatibility between the God of the Old and New Testaments and the gods to whom the knee is bent in modern cultures. The subjectivity possessed in technological cultures poses a barrier to the preaching and hearing of the gospel. Swiftly, Christianity is becoming the religion of the Third world (so-called) and the faith of the Southern Hemisphere. It is further interesting to note that increasing numbers of missionaries are coming to the West to win converts to the way of Jesus Christ.

Now, the point is not to discredit the knowledges that can be acquired by positive methods. There is no advantage, for instance, to removing electricity and eliminating all appliances powered by this force. The same can be said for countless sectors of technological culture. It is, however, to put brackets around positive knowledge, as if it can give a plenary account of possibility. Rather, it is the task of preaching as theology done in and for the pulpit to declare where the boundaries are located. This is nothing other than what the apostle nominated as "demolishing the wisdom of the wise," or "bringing thoughts into captivity to the obedience of Christ" (2 Cor 10:4–5).

It must be noted how the scientific project—both natural and human—have as a propaeduetic the methodological posture of ascertaining what can be known without the "God Hypothesis." This was a reaction to the control the church held over knowledge of every form. Indeed, some of the early investigators of nature by empirical methods were branded and threatened as heretics for teachings about the universe that were deemed to be in conflict with Thomistic metaphysics, know in that day as science. It was not for naught that theology was called the "queen of the sciences."

The bane of science, if not set within appropriate boundaries, is that science itself becomes a form of religion. This is scientism. It is faith in the human mind as the organ of knowledge to penetrate and represent the world in a manner that is plenary. As with Cartesian space, the knower is projected as the referee for truth, with faith that mystery can be driven out and the world can be enlightened by positive projects of investigation. Reason takes the place of God; man becomes the measure; God is but a projection of the human mind.

Now, the issue need not be competition between knowledges—that is, unless a religious approach is taken to both. A clash occurs invariably when the axis is reversed: this is where the approach to science is religious, and the approach to religion is scientific. Then the faith is in science and human potential, and proof is required for the things of faith. The alternative is for scientific and historical knowledges to operate within their domain.

The theological critique must ever be the work of declaring the limited and the plenary domains. A crucial epistemological implication here is acknowledgement of how faith is present in knowledge of any sort. The scriptures speak correctly to say, " . . . by faith we know . . . " By faith we know anything. Without faith, which operates at the presuppositional level, no system of knowledge is so much as set in place. Theorems and proofs can only be made following the assumptions regarding how a system of logic will operate. This knowledge operates within the tacit dimension that precedes proof of any sort.

An example that quickly comes to mind is from the summer of 1969. I was working in a steel prefabrication mill in Atlanta, Georgia. This was the summer of the first walk on the moon. Another young fellow and I were discussing the matter when an elderly gentleman declared forcefully, "Nobody walked on the moon. If God wanted people on the moon, He would have put them there himself." Fresh out of a class in modern physics, I began to give the explanation for how it was possible for a spaceship to go beyond the gravitational pull of the earth, enter the gravitational field of the moon and land. Granted, there would necessarily be some compensation for the difference in gravity, but all this was covered in the explanation.

Well, the old man looked at me, shaking his head. He said, "That's the trouble with you young folk today; you believe everything white folk tell you." I burst into laughter, realizing he had hit the nail on the head. There was no way I could argue with him, giving my explanation, if I had not studied physics. Neither could I convince him of anything if he did not have faith in this way of construing the world.

Quite apart from whether the men walked on the moon or not, my system of knowledge had faith in its very foundation. As such, it is grounded in a "mythos" of its own. That is, it loses all integrity without some account of what is not visible, and how there is mediation between the world of sensible knowledge and what lies behind it. One cannot reason in matters of physics or any other science without learning the "mythos" and "logos" that undergirds it. To put the issue another way, there is no science of physics without a "metaphysic," even if it is nominated as "pure science." There is no chemistry without the mythos of an atomic and subatomic theory of matter. At the zero limit one cannot say with certainty whether the most elementary forms of the world have the character of particles or waves.

In actuality the so-called "scientific account" by which most modern persons live is in essence an "outdated mythos," known as classical physics, and that dates to the latter nineteenth century. By its very presuppositions, anything bearing the resemblance of a "God hypothesis" was excised for the sake of empirical knowledge that could be measured by the sciences and upon which rational persons could agree. That logos worked well within its domain, and it gave rise to many "discoveries" essential to the age of science and technology. However, it left untouched the realm of mystery, which is no less real. It has no answers for the "human challenges" that are equal in terms of primitivity and modernity. It remains inept in the face of micro-organisms that continue to afflict the human body. It is impotent in the conquest of nature, and must still stand in awe in the face of "acts of God."

So then, the work of preaching remains a proclamation of the creative and saving acts of God. But more, it is a declaration of the limited domain of knowledge given to the creature. Even as it draws from these knowledges, preaching ever acknowledges that the mind which receives it is fashioned by the Spirit that gives the very capacity for receiving it. And yet, the mind of the Lord is unknowable, and his ways past finding out.

Block Four: Analysis of the Contemporary Setting

There are times and seasons in the life of the church. Indeed, there is a Christian Year, a Christian Calendar. There is a Year of the Lord, a Year of God's favor. It is not to be confused with mundane time. Even when we speak of "ordinary time," we are not speaking of time that God does not inhabit. Rather, we are talking about the season following Pentecost—the time in which the Spirit fills the church, bringing the people of God under the rule of God. We might even go so far as to call this Whitsuntide, or Kingdomtide. This is the time during which we live in longing and expectation of the reign of God.

Marvelous discursive spaced is opened for preaching when time is observed in the Year of our Lord. This time begins with Advent, continues through Epiphany, is followed by Lent, and is consummated in Easter, and Pentecost. And the cycle begins again.[7]

These nodes, or moments in the cycle, correspond to concrete moments in the life of the gracious dealing of God with the people of his choice and the life and ministry of the Son. As such, they give clues to the concrete moments in the life of the believing community and in the day to day existence of the faithful. As much as any other point of reference, the Christian calendar that marks the Liturgical Year makes preaching real and relevant.

When making preaching real, it is good to observe the "What Principle." To borrow a phrase from the recording artist Les McCann, you make it real compared to "What." For the believer, reality is never merely the narrative supplied by science, history, the succession of kings, or the rise and fall of empires. This is the perishing world from which we are saved in Christ Jesus. Real time and real issues are given to us

---

7. See Lawrence Stookey's *Calendar: Christ's Time for the Church*.

in Christ and in the worship of God. Even where narratives of power and domination cannot be disregarded, they must come under prophetic critique.

Cycles of the local church and the culture are helpful to the extent that they tell us what the people think matters to them. As such, this helps to gain a point of reference in reality. Anniversaries, national holidays, historical moments to remember, cultural accretions that have grown around Christian celebrations provide excellent opportunities to proclaim the gospel against the background with the traction afforded by a critique of culture. This critique need not be the negation of practices cherished by the people. Rather, they can be the point of departure for a deepened understanding of life. In significant ways, the preaching of the gospel is "pointing away from" history as we conceive it to the reality of God given in Christ.

Contemporary issues do not form the substance and content of the gospel. The gospel is the good news of what God has done in Jesus Christ for the salvation of the world. And yet, the contemporary issues plot the locus and perimeter of the world. They show the configuration of a world for which the living God is not central. They manifest the deformations that emerge when God is not glorified. They bring into view the gods of the age—the gods we set before the living God. They reveal where we have bowed and turned ourselves into slaves.

Here the human (or social) sciences can be put into the service of preaching. In this regard they perform their original intent—namely liberating disciplines to unconceal the invisible forces that operate to establish the world we create. They show the human project for what it is. As liberating disciplines they pry open the human mind, which is proclaimed as the organ of knowledge, to disclose its work of imagining the world it goes on to create. The liberating disciplines pinpoint the interests of the subject who has set her self at the center of the world.

Every "ism" has its "mythos" and "logos." The mythos is not obvious. Indeed, it lives by not naming itself or declaring its origin. It persists by not articulating the configuration of power on which it depends. The powers must be named and unmasked in order to be engaged—to use the language of Walter Wink.[8] It is analogous to the exorcisms performed by Jesus, where he commanded the unclean spirits to give their name.

---

8. Wink, *Naming the Powers; Unmaksking the Powers; Engaging the Powers.*

Even then, before they made their exit they "exercised their victims." On one occasion they begged to be given a home in the swine. Following the granting of this petition, they ran the swine headlong over the cliff, revealing their intention for the human body they previously inhabited.

The most pernicious deception of all is when the powers conceal their identity and transmute into legitimate forms of the gospel. It is what the apostle referred to as Satan transforming himself into an angel of light. This occurs whenever "isms" are proclaimed as the gospel. Put another way, it is when the "word of the Lord" is confused with the "word of the land." In the Old Testament this is referred to as false prophecy. It is uttered by those who went forth, but had not been sent by God. They spoke words that were pleasing to the king. But they were under the influence of the lying spirit. What is so unsettling in these accounts (1 Kings 18), the lying spirit is said to have come from God. The occasion was the king who despised the true servant of the Lord and prophets who were his for hire.

Similar admonitions are given in the New Testament, and they can be summarized under the category of the "lying wonder." False prophets, messiahs, and teachers exchange the truth of God for a lie. When the lie is preferred, God gives them up, and the conscience becomes seared. The challenge is to keep the focus on God—the good news of what God has done in Christ, while continuing to point out the diversions from the truth and the delusions that would compete with the truth.

Preaching that performs its given task and "goes somewhere" is driven by relevant questions. Clues for how to raise such questions are given in the scriptures. There is perhaps no question more seminal in this regard than the one asked by Jesus of the disciples in Caeserea Phillipi, namely, "... who do you say that I am?" That is the question that gave rise to the clearest statement of the gospel, namely, "... Thou art the Christ, the Son of the living God" (Matt 16:16–17. Note further that the answer is not given by flesh and blood).

This matter of the relevant question is discussed at great length in the work of S. D. Proctor, who advances what he calls the "dialectical method,"[9] and in other scholars as well. It is given extensive treatment in the work of David Buttrick, who advances the notion of "moves"[10] to

---

9. Proctor, *Certain Sound of the Trumpet* and *How Shall They Hear?*
10. Buttrick, *Homiletic*.

show how preaching is given traction. Specifically, he introduces the notion of the "contrapuntal," which advances the thesis after the opposition has been stated.

Without this traction the sermon stays in one place. It is flat, monotone, inconsequential. In response to it the relevant question is "So what?" Nothing is changed by it. Little if anything is advanced. It is more like a pleasant chat. No one is irritated; nobody is agitated. No one is convicted. No one is healed. Christian preaching demands a response, and supplying traction is crucial in this regard.

One important tool when speaking to one's context is the illustration. Illustration is essential in the sermon. At the same time, however, the purpose of the illustration is to serve the text. The illustration is not a project of its own, and it is not to take on a life of it's own. Without great care in this regard the illustration overpowers the text. This is the decided disadvantage of the long and unwieldy story.

Quite often (I would say, more often than not), the best illustrations come out of the text. This occurs when an image is magnified, or when the action is given in the root meaning of a word. In the case of the Old Testament and the gospels amplification comes through entering the world of the text and "bringing forth" the relevant knowledges required for entering that world. The sheer difference between cultures separated by twenty centuries opens discursive space that is pregnant with potential.

In every case, the space opened by the relevant question shapes the illustration. The thickness—the density, the opacity—of the text is what begs for the shards of light offered by means of illustration. A case study in this regard is the parable of the sower. Here the story of the sower is the illustration of how the word is dispensed. The preparation—or lack thereof—opens the discursive space in which one can see the performance of the word that is dispensed among those who hear the gospel. With "sanctified imagination" one can even hear conversation among the seeds.

It cannot be stated with too much force or repetition that the text shapes the illustration. A good illustration in this regard is that of making duplicate keys. There is the original, with a combination cut into the grooves. It is good for only the tumbler for which it is set. The blank is selected for the closeness of its proximity to the key shape. But the groves are cut into the blank only for the purpose of matching the key combination that is given. A duplicate that takes on its own combination is worthless.

Block Five: Proclamation

The sermon should make clear and direct proclamation of the gospel of God. No matter what else may or must be done for clarity, relevance, and engagement of the congregation, what must not be excised is proclamation.

Christian preaching is first and foremost about God. Immediately, more needs to be said about the world God created—a world God has not ceased to love. Much is to be said concerning the creature in the image of God—deliverance, chastisement, restoration, defense from the hand of the enemy. But the centerpiece of the story is God. Note that this is the very structure of the Apostle's Creed, and any others that are noteworthy in the church. The faith is in the Father Almighty, the son Jesus Christ, and the Spirit who proceeds from the Father.

At the same time, preaching a text is not a claim about God in general. Neither is necessarily a certain set of teachings. It is the word declared in and by a particular text. It is what the Spirit has to say to the church through a given lection. Such attention to the text for what to proclaim expands knowledge of God from a set of delivering acts isolated and narrated from the past, when needs of equal or greater magnitude can be met through attention to the specific text.

It is true that Jesus got up from the grave—early one morning, and with the victory over death and hell. But that is not the gospel to be declared at the expense of what is given for the day to be set before the people—in 1 John 3:1–2, for example. If we believe the word is living—quick, powerful, sharper than a two-edge sword—we are empowered to take up what is given—or, should I say, take it up where we find it.

A superb skill for the preacher to develop is that of "tuning in on the gospel" found in a specified lection. Otherwise, there is a distinct tendency to short-change the people in search of what we desire, or "what God has laid on my heart." Some of the greatest gospel comes from some of the most difficult and trying texts. This is a good word that would be missed without the discipline of hearing what a specified text has to say.

Undermining a text in favor of other truth is a bane of much preaching. Quite often this is done in the name of "preaching the word." The measure of how faithfully one has preached the word is not given in the number of texts that are cited. It is possible for texts to be set in opposition to one another. Just as bad is "quenching the word" in one passage by skipping to another before the given word has time to speak. Standing before the mystery, waiting for the word to speak, listening for the voice of God in a given lection is a skill and spiritual discipline worth developing for the sake of those God would save.

The same undermining can occur in preaching that "goes out of the way" to "condemn sin." What can result is the preacher's condemnation of what displeases him or her. I will ever recall the confession of a great preached who had it in for smokers, in part because he was formed in a tradition which taught that smoking is sin. He said on one occasion when he had railed against the smokers, the Lord asked him: "Did you preach that sermon because you hate smoking or because you love me?"

On another occasion I was quizzed on whether I preach on homosexuality. I wasn't sure how to answer such a question. When I finally preached through Romans, I realized why. It was as if the text 'interrogated" me about how I preach in these matters. I found guidance from preaching the text rather than "tackling the issue" as it is framed in popular discourse. As it happened, the issue that came forth from the text was whether Christ is Lord over the body. If the answer is no, there are serious problems for preaching the gospel. If the answer is yes, there are many matters that must be address for a life of consistent submission to the Lordship of Christ. Some interests of the contemporary church should not be set aside for isolated treatment at the expense of how they are set within a matrix of a larger array in matters of soteriology. Put another way, there is far greater benefit in letting the text speak and listening to what the word has to say than in framing the issue first and demanding answers in a prescribed format.

Where the text is clear one can and should be bold to declare what has been given. Once again, however, exegetical and theological tools are essential. Without them one can scarcely distinguish between what the text has to say and the constructions of the text that pre-exist within the traditions of the church. Scarcely can one find in any segments of the church those who outright disclaim the scriptures as their authority. That is, Christians do not announce themselves as "unscriptural."

And yet there are many believers and traditions that do not lay claim to or take responsibility for the theology done by them or for them. This is especially the case within Protestant traditions that claim "sola scriptura." As one group puts it, they have no creed but Christ, no doctrine but the bible. The phrase sounds catchy and on the surface appears inviting. But the truth is that these believers do the same as everyone else in the matters of preaching, teaching, interpreting, and ordering the life of the church.

Good preaching is done so as to make the authority perspicuous. It confronts people with their own authority—that is, the authority they have already accepted. It is nothing short of a waste of time to interpret and proclaim in a manner that retreats from the authority given within a tradition and to impose one that is extraneous.

An example in this regard goes a long way. Louis Farrakan is fond of quoting Christian scripture, telling Christians what they (we) believe. But he is loose and free with the methods and traditions of interpretation current among Christians. While he may have much to say that is critical of modern culture, and while his words may have deep resonance among faithful Muslims, the authority is limited where the authority for his interpretation is not recognized.

Christian preaching is for a purpose. It is not merely sound and fury, signifying nothing. The preacher does not speak for her self; nor does he speak merely to hear his voice. Rather, preaching is speech for God; it is to accomplish a purpose. The word is not sent to return void, but to accomplish what it is sent to perform.

Preaching performs the work of proclamation of the reign of God. It calls for repentance—that is, turning from the power of Satan to the kingdom of the dear Son. It calls for a turn from the life of sin and bondage to a life of freedom in the Spirit. It serves the purpose of teaching the faith for the formation of disciples. It deepens faith, so those who believe may know what power is made available through Christ Jesus, who breathes out the Spirit among the believers.

The word of preaching sanctifies through the truth. That is, after planting the seed of faith in the believing heart, it brings on a correspondence within the members, causing the body to become obedient—indeed, an instrument of righteousness. So it is that preaching that is to be taken seriously is itself an act of expectation (anticipation) to behold what God would work within the body.

And preaching is itself an act of worship. It is not separate from the liturgy. One is hard-pressed to say that it is even the highlight of the liturgy. It is an ingredient—indispensable, without substitute. It is not a word spoken from above, but from within the midst of the people. Although set apart for the work, the preacher is one from among the people with whom she worships.

The possible contradiction is stated well in a poem we learned as children. It went like this:

> The parish priest of austerity went into a high church steeple
>
> To be near to God, so he could he could send his word down on the people.
>
> In sermon script he daily wrote what he thought was sent from heaven,
>
> And passed it down on the people's heads three times one day in seven.
>
> In his old age God spoke and said 'come down and die.' And he cried from the steeple, "Where art thou Lord?' And the Lord replied, 'Down here among the people.'

The preacher who is not a worshipper strikes a dissonant note. The same can be said of the preacher who is dispassionate, unmoved, not affected by the word declared or the people to whom it is declared. The formation of the liturgy is crucial for bringing forth the word that does not stand alone. The prayers, the reading of the word, the acts of praise prepare the hearts of the people for what is delivered. There are instances in which a particularly difficult word cannot penetrate or be heard without elaborate preparation of the people by the Spirit. Like the hard ground of the footpath in the parable, such a word is picked up by the birds of the air, or thrown back by the hearer who has difficulty receiving it. With different preparation that same word can bring forth much fruit.

Even though elaborate preparation must be made on the part of the preacher, and highly technical skills are required for preparation and delivery, it is received by the people in "whole form." In the moment of analysis it can be dissected and critiqued in matters of form and structure. But in the moment when it is being done, preaching is a whole act, an ingredient in worship, and engagement of the intellect and the emotions.

I will ever recall instances when I have played sermon tapes for an introductory class in preaching. Along with the monitor, the script from which the sermon was delivered was put in the hands of the students. Some were more absorbed by the monitor; others by the script. Of great interest to me was the fact that those who gave more attention to the script thought the sermon was too complicated. Those looking at the monitor and watching the people claimed it was too emotional.

The point was made precisely: the sermon does both. It feeds and challenges the mind. At the same time, it moves the hearer to doxology. The response is to be praise, celebration, deepened faith, renewed commitment to service. The word of preaching is not to return void.

PART II The Practice of Preaching

four THE WORD OF FAITH

But what saith it? The word is nigh thee, even in thy mouth, and in thy heart: that is the word of faith, which we preach: That if thou shalt confess with thy mouth the Lord Jesus, and shalt believe in thine heart that God hath raised him from the dead, thou shalt be saved (Rom 10:8–9).

We are not permitted to so much as ask the question, "Who shall ascend into heaven to bring Christ down, or who shall descend to raise him from the dead?" No, we are not so much as to ask this in our heart. So what shall we say? What does the word say? What is the word we may speak? Like the tutor he was, the Apostle Paul taught the lessons of salvation. Here we are challenged with the lesson of faith. This is the word he preached. We do well to know it. The word of faith is what we preach.

This word is near to us—as near as the mouth. It is located at this primary point of entrance to the body. At this orifice we take in the very substances that enable us to live. We speak those words that enhance life or sound the knell of death. When the word of faith fills the mouth, it enters the body and permeates the entire being. It takes the space other words are vying to fill—words of doubt and discouragement, words of cursing or comfort.

The word of faith is a word that imparts knowledge. Much is made of the knowledge that comes only by faith. According to Hebrews, by faith we know the worlds were framed by the word of his power. The truth of the matter is that all knowledge comes by faith. There is no system of knowledge that can progress with the minutest movement in the absence of presuppositions. Even with the "so-called" facts of math, we can have no confidence in our addition unless we assume or set a base. Change the base from 10 to 7, and 4 + 4 is no longer 8. There is much more to be said in this regard, and we will get to it in time.

This word is put in our mouth, and for this we are wise to give thanks. The word from the Lord, the word of faith is not the only word being heard in the land. In the political realm, there is the word of war. In pop culture, there is a word that has no use for the word of faith we are given to preach. Even among the churches one can hear contrary words. Just what are the words we are preaching? And when one hears contrary words, how will they know how to decide? Either directly or through acquiescence, we teach words along with the music that is being ingested. These can be words of pessimism, hedonism, sexism, and nihilism. They enter the mouth and the ear. How can it be that they do not influence the heart? The word we need is the word that has been given. It is the word of faith that we preach.

During this Advent Season there is no theme we could accent with more profit than the "nearness of God." This is the meaning of the name "Emmanuel." God is near us in the word made flesh in the Son. He is God incarnate, touching our infirmities, healing our diseases, redeeming our lives from destruction. In the Son, God is near us to infiltrate these clay vessels. He assumed our humanity that we might partake of his divinity. This is all so that we might be saved. In all this wonderful work, the word of faith is at the core.

The word of faith is authored by the Spirit, who puts it in the mouth. This is a word of faith, not foolishness. It is not a matter of being outrageous and preposterous. This word is not to be confused with a god complex, where we speak reality into existence. No, we are not given the power that belongs to God. We are no more trustworthy than Lucifer. Only God speaks by fiat. The word of faith is not some baptized version of abracadabra. Rather, the word of faith results from our being carried into the world of God, and having our wills so conformed.

The word of faith is not detached from the work it is given to perform. It proceeds from the mouth of God to our mouth, as with a divine kiss. What is spoken corresponds to what is planted in the heart. This is unlike the servant who said, "I will go into the vineyard," but never went. The word of faith produces works, or else it is dead.

In all of this, the datum is salvation. It is not about what I want in advance of God implanting righteous desires. True, God can bless whom

God wills. But we are not talking about "speaking our way" into a 10,000 square foot house when we can't take care of 2,000 square feet. The word of faith is not about speaking your way into a Jag or a Porsche, when you are struggling to make the payment on the Ford. No, God teaches us to be faithful over a few things before making us the ruler over many. Putting the word of faith into our mouth is about bringing us into the will of God, so that we desire the ways of life and salvation. If God is having trouble with me in my Chevrolet, what makes me think I will be so much more productive for the kingdom if I own a private Jet?

The word of faith is not a matter of cute sayings and fancy rhymes. I'm not so sure about sayings like, "I'm too blessed to be stressed . . . too anointed to be disappointed . . ." I don't know whether that is faith or not. There is a blessing in being able to live under stress. Just as sure as you live, you will come under stress, whether you claim it or not, whether you call it by another name or not. Sickness is real, even for those who trust in God. The same is so with heartache and bereavement. There are times when the very anointing upon our lives will leave us in a state of disappointment. When you know the power of God like the apostle, you want everyone to taste his goodness—especially your kinsmen. The Anointed One was disappointed by his people to the point where he wept over the city that did not know the day of her visitation. No, the word of faith is a deposit of the Spirit that causes us to know when the word is right, even though it be refused.

The word of faith is given in a language of confidence, patience, persistence, and victory. It is not a matter of games and gimmicks. Faith is not measured by the price tag on the line in which you stand. My faith is not greater than yours because I stand in a $50 blessing line, and the one you stand in is set at a rate of only $25. You don't show your faith by running up to the altar and throwing your money in a bucket while the preacher is preaching. Faith is not to be equated with foolishness. You don't prove another's faith by getting them out of the bed during terminal illness and making them run around the room. Stop taking your medicine at your own risk, but don't blame your demise on God. Don't even say it has anything to do with the amount of faith. Withdraw all of your money from the bank and default on your mortgage if you dare, but when you lose your house like that, don't count on staying with me.

I will forever recall the time when a friend asked me to go see a man who was not recovering as he should, due to depression. He was a minister who had quadruple bypass surgery, and all the medical signs said he should have been doing fine. The problem was that he had friends like Job. They went into his room to chastise him for not exercising his faith and taking the surgery in stride. He told me that to do the procedure they had to take out his heart, keep him alive on a machine, and make the repairs. My question to him was, if he had not exercised faith what had he done? I prayed for him to be delivered from the spirit of depression. But most of all I prayed for him to be delivered from friends who were teaching "false faith."

The word of faith comes by the teaching of the Holy Ghost, who causes us to know the difference between carnal things and spiritual things. Only the Spirit can teach us to speak the good confession that Jesus is Lord. We say it with the mouth in a manner that corresponds to the inward motions of the heart. This is the first step in learning a new language, which corresponds to a new walk. It is speaking in a manner that is consistent with the scriptures. It inaugurates a new walk that ushers us into a new realm of truth.

There is no better time for this word to come to us than Advent. Advent is about God coming near to us in the Son. He is God from God, light from light. By the incarnation, the Son has assumed our nature, and he is touched with the feeling of our infirmities. In him the very God has infiltrated our vessel. By assuming our humanity he has provided for us to partake of the divine nature. And this is so that we might be saved. Saved from sin, saved from wrath, saved from our selves, saved from a wicked generation, saved to bring others to salvation, saved to fulfill the purpose for which we were created. He saves me from every sin and harm, secures my soul each day; I'm leaning strong on his mighty arm, I know He'll guide me all the way. Saved by his power divine.

Confessing the Lord Jesus is more than saying a word as an empty speech act. It is rejecting Caesar as Lord. In the time of the early church, this was one of the most seditious acts that could be committed in the Roman Empire. The powers understood it well. It was rebellion, and it was regarded as such. Accordingly, confessing Jesus as Lord was the cause for great persecution. Emperors blurred their identity with that of the deities. They extended the work of the empire as the work of God. They claimed divine blessing for their expansion, their murder, and their subjugation of nations. They brutally put down any rebellion.

Rejection of imperial authority was viewed as seriously as taking up arms against the empire. In a sense it may have been an even greater threat. For if the lie were ever exposed, there was no telling who might follow the same pattern. Confessing that Jesus is Lord put the emperor in the same category as Lucifer, who sought to set his throne above the throne of God, or the King of Tyre, in whom iniquity was found. Believers in the Lord Jesus knew that kings rise and fall as the mere exchange of thrones. But Christ is the maker of all things, visible and invisible. His kingdom reigns from shore to shore till moon shall wax and wane no more.

The word of faith: O that troublesome word. It does not ask who shall ascend to bring Christ down. It does not calculate how it shall be when the Lord has spoken it. Rather, the Spirit puts it in the mouth, even as he put it in the body of Mary, showing that nothing is impossible for God. It is placed in the mouth to impede the weak word, even if prayer for help with unbelief must follow it. The Spirit puts this word in the mouth to impede the doubting word, the foul word, the curse word, the dissembling word.

The word of faith releases power, for it confesses the Lordship of Jesus. There is power in the name; there is healing in the name. At the name of Jesus every knee must bow. Devils tremble at the name; principalities submit. Jesus praised Peter for uttering the word that confessed him, declaring that flesh and blood had not revealed it to him, even though he had to rebuke Peter for the weak word that followed.

Can anybody remember how they taught us to call his name when we were "praying through"? Does anybody know the name—the precious name? The saints knew what life had in store for us. In that moment of seeking, when our hearts were tender, they taught us that if we persistently called the name, heaven would move, and there would be a corresponding movement inside of us. We thought we were through, but they said, "Keep calling him baby." And so we did till we had the witness—the assurance that no power could shake. Ever so often I find myself resorting to that same discipline learned at the altar. When temptations round me gather, I breathe the holy name in prayer.

Learn the language of confession. There are times when you can't figure out what is going on around you. The kingdoms rage, the powers hiss, the rage of Satan is evident. You need the salvation of the Lord. Learn how to confess him. Say with the Psalmist, "The Lord is my shepherd" (Ps 23). Speak with the prophet, "But now thus saith the Lord that created you, O Jacob, and he that formed thee, O Israel, Fear not: for I have redeemed thee" (Isa 43:1). Confess with the hymn writers:

> Jesus, the name high over all
> In hell or earth or sky;
> angels and men before it fall,
> and devils fear and fly.[1]

> He looks, and ten thousands of angels rejoice,
> and myriads wait for his word;
> He speaks, and eternity filled with his voice
> Re-echoes the praise of the Lord.[2]

And this is where Advent and the Table take us: to the proclamation of the Lord's suffering and death until he comes. What's more, the requirement for coming to the Table is the test of worthiness—namely, whether we believe it, whether we make the good confession. The examination is not whether we are perfect, flawless, without fault. It is whether we confess his Lordship, or whether we flirt with other lords. Even making an error can be an acceptance of his Lordship, of his authority to correct, to chastise, to say what course we should have taken. Jesus is the way, the truth, and the life.

See, O see the wonderful correlation between receiving the word in our mouth and being fed at the Table of the Lord. To make the good confession, we receive the living word. At the Table we are fed the food of faith. It is not the matter, but the faith in God that is the substance. By faith we receive the word, and all the sweet tokens of pardoning grace, as nourishment for the soul. And this itself is proclamation of the Lord's death until he comes. Even now he reigns, and all powers and authorities shall be put under his feet, and we shall feast anew in the kingdom.

The word of faith is in our mouth, even as the broken bread. The bread of life, not the stone of the wilderness; the bread of life, not the ser-

---

1. Charles Wesley, "Jesus! The Name High Over All," 1749.
2. Joseph Swain, "O Thou in Whose Presence," 1791.

pent from a begrudging father. His broken body is a gift to us, not some reward we earn. So we do not come to the Table with any sort of attitude. We don't slide from the table of demons to come to this table; nor do we come to it from our orgies. We do not come drunk, gouging, or without love and charity for our brothers and sisters. We don't come mean, mad, or not believing. This is the Table of our Lord. We come by invitation; we honor it as his table. We do not do him a favor; we receive favor.

And so we partake of his body and blood. We receive the word in our mouth; we eat it; we confess our Lord. He said, "I am the living bread that came down from heaven. . . . Unless you eat the flesh and of the Son of Man and drink his blood, you have no life in you" (John 6:51, 53 NRSV). The space we inhabit at the Table reserves our room in the kingdom of the Son. He reigns forever and evermore. Jesus is Lord.

five   GOING TO THE OUTER LIMITS

That if thou shalt confess with thy mouth the Lord Jesus, and shalt believe in thine heart that God hath raised him from the dead, thou shalt be saved. For with the heart man believeth unto righteousness; and with the mouth confession is made unto salvation (Rom 10:9–10).

With these verses we remain at the very heart of the mystery of salvation. Here is where it throbs; this is where the wondrous work of God is poured forth into the life of the ransomed. Our Christ is the lamb slain from before the foundation of the world. He has redeemed us to God by his blood, and he is worthy to receive blessing, and wisdom, and honor, and riches, and glory. To him be dominion forever and forever. And yet, this wondrous work is for me; it is for you. The appropriation takes place in a simple act of faith. The word of faith is put in our mouth and our heart. With the mouth, we confess that Jesus is Lord. With the heart, we believe unto righteousness.

This word is good all the time. Indeed, this is the gospel—the good news of what God has done. He has translated us from the kingdom of Satan to the kingdom of the dear Son, and given us an inheritance among those who are sanctified through faith in Christ Jesus. Yet, the season of Advent accents the goodness and the beauty of this word. In the midst of the spending and the merriment—and in spite of the failed ventures to turn the season into a generic holiday—those who believe insist that it is about the Son of God who was born in a manger. Christmas is celebration of Christ. New life, new hopes to all he brings. He is the way, the truth, and the life. The greatest gift is the Son. By the Spirit comes the gift of faith, whereby with the heart we believe unto righteousness.

Odd as it may seem, the word we have before us today can overwhelm us with its simplicity. It stands to reason that if the gift of salvation is so great, there must be something great we must do. Yet all we are instructed to do is believe on the Lord Jesus. It seems like we ought to have to do more. That is precisely the dilemma with which the Apostle is struggling. He is battling with kinsmen who would accuse him of oversimplifying the matter. They were zealous for the law. In their zeal, they accused him of nullifying it and transgressing the truth revealed to Moses.

Paul insisted that attempting to do more than believe is actually doing less. In believing we submit to the Eternal God who gives the power to keep the law. Indeed, the Son has kept it, performing the righteousness the Father requires. This is righteousness we cannot produce. But by the Spirit a mystery is performed in the believing heart that brings forth the righteousness that fulfills the law. The yield is a life of obedience, witness, and all the sacrifice the human creature is incapable of producing on its own.

But here comes the pivot of it all. It is not a matter of faith in general; it is not believing in a God who *was*. One is not talking here of a God who is locked in antiquity, or who is known only through laws and rites that have been given. No, saving faith is in the God who was, is, and is to come. This God is Abba—the Father of the Lord Jesus, the God who raised him from the dead. This is the God who we cannot set within boundaries, and concerning whom we have no say-so in the matter of what is possible. It is He who has made us, and not we ourselves. He breathed the breath of life into Adam in creation. By the Spirit he fashioned the body of obedience for the Son and placed him in the womb of Mary. By the Spirit of life he touched the Son, who obeyed by offering himself in death. Through the Eternal Spirit he secured our redemption and reigns in glory. The Spirit supplies us with faith to believe in our heart that God raised him, and this gives us communion with him. And this is what it means to be saved: fellowship with the Risen Christ in the Spirit.

This is the hurdle, for Paul's day and for ours. He split the Sanhedrin in half when they sought to try him. He knew what he was doing, and it worked. He told them he was on trial for believing in the resurrection of the dead. Sadducees rushed to the judgment that he must have been a bad fellow, drunk with his knowledge, which was grounded in an error. Pharisees, who believed in the resurrection in general, said there should be no such rush to judgment. But even they could not stomach the thought that God had raised the one who exposed their hypocrisy and preached deliverance to the captives. Paul declared to the learned ones at Corinth that if Christ is not raised from the dead our faith is in vain, we are yet in our sins, and we are among men most miserable.

O yes, there were Jews who believed Jesus was a good man, a prophet of God, a Messiah worth following. But they couldn't go all the way and confess that God raised him from the dead. There are some to this day who are ethically conscientious and morally good. But they have difficulty making the radical confession on which Paul insists. They cannot make the full confession with the Ancient Church. They can say, "I believe in God the Father Almighty, maker of heaven and earth, and in Jesus Christ his only Son our Lord." But they back up at the point of saying the Son "was conceived of the Holy Ghost, born of the virgin Mary, suffered under Pontius Pilate, he descended into hell; the third day he rose from the dead and sitteth at the right hand of God the Father Almighty."

But either you believe this or you don't. You cannot make yourself believe it. You cannot argue your way to this datum in faith; there is no rational process to get you there; there is no logical exercise to keep you a believer. This is the word of faith the Spirit puts in the mouth and plants in the heart. No one can confess that Jesus is Lord except by the Spirit. From the other side, when the heart believes, there is no power that can extract this faith from us.

The apostle knows where he is when he deals with this dynamic of the believing heart. Ah, he was possessed with wisdom from on high. See how he couples together incarnation and the resurrection at the very outset of the epistle in making his declaration of authority. The gospel unto which he was separated is rooted in the promises of the prophets in the holy scriptures, and it concerned the Son Jesus Christ our Lord, "which was made of the seed of David according to the flesh; and declared to be the Son of God with power, according to the spirit of holiness, by the resurrection from the dead" (1:3–4).

See, both the incarnation and the resurrection lie on the same boundary of knowledge. In both cases the issue is epistemological: that is, it has to do with what is knowable, and how we know. Within every civilization there is some logic to knowledge, by which we can have agreements about what is true, what makes sense, what can be believed, what is compelling. Within the last few days there have been several convictions in high profile murder cases. In one case the prosecutor argued concerning what is logically incredible. That is, it didn't make sense to say that a woman five feet two inches tall could stretch high enough to shoot through the opening where the bullet must have passed to hit the victim. The jury convicted the former state trooper. This was strictly on the grounds of what is reasonable—what is believable on logical grounds. The best attorneys are good logicians.

Well, with Paul we have an excellent logician. Not only does he make explorations within the logical limits of Jewish thought; he carries us to the limit. For the bottom line in any system of knowledge is what is even possible. And that is where the tentmaker sets up his tent. He bids us to come to the outer limits of our knowledge—whatever the system might be. The boundary is creation, incarnation, and resurrection. When you talk about the Son Jesus Christ our Lord, the discourse is framed around the question of possibility. In so many words he is saying: in order to talk about salvation we must deal with the more fundamental question of what can and can't be done. The question is whether anything is too hard for God. If so, the next question is what kind of God are we talking about? If we speak of the living God, then all things are possible.

One of the biggest problems we have in our day is trying to believe with our head in the things of God because we have already believed with our heart the things of science. There are only a few true scientists. But there are thousands who believe in electricity, automobiles, cell phones, X-rays, and the whole array of medical technology. I will never forget how I argued with a man in Atlanta in 1969 when he told me nobody went to the moon. He said to me, "the trouble with you young folk is that you believe everything white folk tell you." I realized in that moment how I had believed the presuppositions and theories of physics in order to make my argument for how a spaceship could thrust past the gravitational pull of the earth. Don't get me wrong; there is some element of faith in any system of knowledge, and I am grateful for scientific advances. But the question is, what faith is ruling your heart?

The great wonder in salvation is the work of grace whereby the Spirit takes over the rule of the heart and enables it to believe the word of faith. The heart is the seat and center where there is unity among perceiving, thinking, knowing, willing, and engagement of the body. When the heart believes, we know there are no limits with God. We are translated into another domain; it is the dominion of the Risen Lord. There he has freedom with our heart to do with it what the prophets promised—he transforms it from one that is stony, deceitful, wicked, and rebellious. He writes a new law, gives a new desire, and imparts new knowledge. The Spirit removes resistance, releases energy, floods the heart with love, and fulfills it through obedience.

Believing in the heart is not to be equated with faith in foolishness. We believe that God raised Jesus from the dead. Death, not a coma; death, not a deep sleep; death, not some fantasy where a stunt man took his place on the cross. Christ is not Tom Cruise. We believe God conquered death and all the powers of hell when he raised the Son. All principalities, powers, and thrones are under his feet. The Risen Christ has the dominion. He has power to rule my heart and all my passions. He has power to guide my future. Believing in the heart brings on the correspondence between what is confessed with the mouth and what is practiced in the body. Being saved is more than shaking hands and getting wet. It is more than singing, clapping, jumping, and jerking when we are in the building. It is being ordered through the heart by the one who has the dominion.

With the heart we believe unto righteousness—that is, the heart believes God raised Jesus from the dead. With your head you can believe some of anything and become a fool. You can't believe this with your heart and remain the same. When you believe on the Lord Jesus you are a changed woman, a changed man. You can't go back and remain the same. The taste of the heavenly gift and the joy of the world to come are too wonderful. No, I won't turn back. "I'm pressing on the upward way."[1]

We believe unto righteousness. This is the righteousness of faith. Our righteousness is not set out before us, as was the case with the law. Rather, the righteousness is in the resurrected Christ. It is given to us through the communion of the Spirit. In him we cross a threshold that opens into an inexhaustible source of vitality and power. Our energy does not go into an obsession with keeping regulations; it is given in submission and obedience.

By the resurrection a great reversal has taken place. In the resurrection, life comes forth from the midst of death. Death is defeated; it is overcome; it is swallowed up in victory. It is stripped of its power to sepa-

---

1. The first line of Johnson Oatman Jr.'s hymn, "Higher Ground," 1898.

rate from God. The sting gone, it has no power to intimidate. Faithfulness to God is not limited by resistance and opposition. In breaking the grip of sin and evil, power is released for obedience. In the subjugation of the powers there is an increase in the resources for faithful service.

What comes to mind is the sources we have for fuel that supplies powerful machines. For the most part, we no longer rely on human beings and animals for the greatest exercise of power. No, we turn to reserves in the earth. We refer to them as fossil fuels. Scientists tell us these deposits are traceable to plant life from past millennia. Dead and decayed vegetation give back the energy absorbed from the sun and the earth in coal, oil, and gas reserves that is retrieved by mining and drilling. It is refined in a usable form on which our civilization relies.

Here we see an apt comparison for what it means to believe unto righteousness. By the resurrection of the Son, we draw on the sources that are deposited in the defeat of death and its allies. Power comes through overcoming death. The trial now makes us stronger; resistance is transformed into courage. We are at a new place now. We live from the fossil fuel of the defeated foes.

Each victory helps us to win some other. Every time we turn around he makes a way; he turns midnight into day. He takes what was meant for evil and brings forth good. Puny faith becomes powerful faith. The faltering heart becomes a faithful heart. With the heart we believe unto righteousness. "Lord I want to be a Christian in my heart: I want to be more holy; I want to be like Jesus in my heart."[2]

This is a confrontation over the question of what is possible. The issue is whether we make the definition or whether we submit to the righteousness of God. If we make the definition, we are sure to fail. We will keep the laws we prefer and make excuses for those we don't like. We will fashion our righteousness in a way that allows us to judge others. Or, we will turn ourselves into hypocrites, pretending to keep laws we break routinely. The saddest consequence is the frustration we cause or encounter for failure to submit. When we submit to the righteousness of God, our heart is enabled to believe. We receive a donation of faith from the domain in which the Risen Christ rules.

When I look at what Paul is doing, my mind goes back to a television program that used to come on during the sixties, I believe. It was a

2. From the American folk hymn, "Lord, I Want to Be a Christian."

Rod Serling production called "The Outer Limits." The music was weird, and it was an invitation to come out of one's comfort zone in knowledge and to explore what it might mean to cross boundaries of time, perception, and expectation. So you might have one show where Benjamin Franklin or a cowboy from the nineteenth century was projected into the twentieth century. Technology commonplace at mid-century was experienced as weird and strange, often prompting the desire to return to the previous era. Mind you, that was some forty years ago, when our culture had not begun to comprehend the convenience (or should I say the inconvenience) of the cell phone and the Internet. A whole lot of us haven't quite caught up to the twenty-first century, and some of us only do what we must. Ever so often we need perspective brought to bear to make us aware of when we are operating within limited domains.

Paul steps in front of Rod Serling, as he takes us to the outer limit so that we can be saved. His desire for his brethren and for us is that we might be saved. The frame for this discourse is a circumference that plots the points as salvation, knowledge, righteousness, incarnation and resurrection. Christ has already descended as the incarnate Son; he has already ascended as the risen Son.

We cross a boundary and enter another domain when we are saved. We do this by believing with our heart. We have access to the outer limits, and we are no longer bound in the domain where sin reigns. The outer limits become interior transcendence. That's what it means to be saved—immediate access, constant communion.

When all is said and done, Christmas is about the outer limits; it is about salvation. It is a celebration of the birth of Jesus. And why is his name Jesus? The Holy Scriptures leave us no room for doubt in the matter. When Joseph would have put the girl away quietly, an angel of the Lord appeared to him in a dream, taking him to the outer limits. The holy child was conceived by the Holy Ghost, and he need not fear taking her. He reached to the outer limits for his name: the Lord is salvation. His name is Jesus, for he shall save his people from their sins. He gave him a name that is above every name.

Buy gifts, deck the halls; most anybody can do that. But be sure to go to the outer limits. His name is Jesus. Call on his name. Go to the outer limits in praise.

six   THE SUPPRESSED SIDE OF CHRISTMAS

For the scripture saith, Whosoever believeth on him shall not be ashamed. ... For whosoever shall call upon the name of the Lord shall be saved (Rom 10:11–13).

So Christ was once offered to bear the sins of many; and unto them that look for him shall he appear the second time without sin unto salvation (Heb 9:28).

I have been giving thought, like many others, to the running debate concerning how to celebrate publicly during this season of the year. The questions have to do with how to name activities, what scenes to use, what are specifically Christian symbols, whether to sing carols or seasonal songs. One groups argues that apart from the Christian celebration of the birth of Christ there would be no reason for the season. Another group argues that the celebration has morphed into a cultural event, and retaining specifically Christian language and symbols alienates persons of other faiths and persons of no faith. A commentator said the other day that with the outcome of the last presidential election, evangelical Christians have been emboldened in their stance. In one case a suit was filed to insure that a Nativity Scene be displayed in public. In another case there was an add admonishing Christians not to purchase from merchants who refused to use the language "Merry Christmas."

Pondering these verses from Romans pushed me further to the last verse from Hebrews 9, where my perspective in the matter has been clarified. Celebrating the coming of Christ is not socially or politically neutral. The texture of the Christian claim is thick. More is at stake than many Christians realize. We who believe on the Lord Jesus and accept the promises of the holy prophets would do well to accept the angst caused by Christmas and admit that it is more than a cultural festival. Indeed, Christmas has a side that the church in the affluent West tends to suppress.

There is a side to Christmas that is anything but "merry" to those who are not in Christ. Not only does it leave out, it offends those who reject Jesus as the king born in a manger. Celebrated rightly, Christmas pronounces judgment and conviction upon those who oppress the poor and pervert justice. Joy is for those who confess Jesus as Lord. Or, there can be joy for suppressing the reign of righteousness in favor of a generic holiday.

O the irony of it all! For the economic sector, Christmas is over on Christmas Eve. The Malls closed early on Friday. K-Mart, and perhaps another one or two stores stayed open till eight o'clock for stragglers. The other merchants had done their work, received their reward, and begun plans for another season. For those who believe on Jesus the party is only beginning. Christmas Eve is the end of Advent. Now is the time for our rejoicing, not only for the birth of a baby in a manger, but for the celebration of Christ's lordship over heaven and earth.

The light comes from the star of Bethlehem that the shepherds saw. The giving of gifts reflects the reverence of the Three Maji who searched for the baby. But Herod knew there was more. Isn't it ironic that the one who would spoil the party is the one who grasped the true gravity? He asked for the location of the baby so he could worship. But his worship would have removed Jesus from the scene. Herod was keen with regard to the side our generation prefers to suppress. But we dare not follow that course in the Church of the Living God, the pillar and ground of truth. For great is the mystery of godliness we profess: God was manifest in the flesh, justified in the Spirit, seen of angels, preached unto the Gentiles, believed on in the world, received up into glory. And we dare not suppress it.

"Whosoever believeth on him shall not be ashamed," quotes the apostle. This suggests that there shall be shame for those who do not call on him. Again, he says that those who call on the name of the Lord shall be saved. He continues with his litany of questions concerning how they can call on him of whom they have not heard. And there is more to say in this matter. But for now, look carefully at these matters of believing and calling on the name of the Lord.

There is a call that comes from the believing heart. This is the one who has heard in faith, which is a gift the Spirit plants within the heart. The result is a nourishing, life-giving communion in the Spirit. This is what it means to be saved: it is life wherein one partakes of the divine nature through the atonement of the Son. The shame of disbelief is taken, the stain of sin is removed, and the sting of death is healed. But more, God's future of righteousness is embraced, and so is his judgment of the world that resists his rule.

The apostle knew very well what it means to pass from one domain to the other. Put another way, he was familiar in an intimate manner with the spirit of Herod, which continued to infect many of his kinsmen. Some would come to the point where they called on the name of Jesus, but they would forever bear the shame of their unbelief. Like him, they would spend the rest of their lives tearing down those works that had been wrought against Christ. Or, there would be those who lived a life of disobedience to face their works in judgment, when compelled to look on their Savior whom they had pierced. This is where the name of the Lord is called unto shame, and not unto salvation.

Some hear a hint of "universalism" in these verses and argue that in God's time all shall be saved, and none shall be lost. A debate rages at present among some of the most popular preachers in the country concerning this matter. True, the Risen Lord has the keys to death, hell, and the grave; and he has not given those keys to us. The keys we have been given are the keys to the kingdom. The key is to confess the Lord Jesus.

Our calling is not to religious bigotry or self-righteous snobbery. At the same time, we are not given some general, amorphous, inter-religious goulash for our spiritual food. Don't count on getting in through the back door; that is the entrance for the thief and the robber. The gospel we have been given is not encouragement for people to take chances with their soul; it is to believe and be baptized for the remission of sins. There is a scandal at the manger. There is a suppressed side that must be proclaimed.

The prophetic dimension to the message and meaning of Christmas comes to the fore when Christ is at the center. It is stated clearly and forcefully in the Song of Mary—the *Magnificat*. She sang, "He hath put down the mighty from their seats, and exalted them of low degree. He hath filled the hungry with good things; and the rich he hath sent empty away." But the prophecy did not stop there; it continued with Simeon and Anna. Simeon declared the sword that would pierce through Mary's soul, and Anna declared the redemption for those who looked to him in faith. The mystery is about the salvation of the world. But there is a suppressed side that is bound with redemption and judgment.

What if we truly celebrated Christ rather than quibbling over how to nominate the holiday, or rather than looking for the minimum offense? The progression is from the manger to the eschaton. There is the review of the themes through the cross and resurrection to the return of the Lord to establish his rule of justice. A glance to the past is helpful in this regard. See how heavily the church has drawn on the language of Revelation as much as that of the gospels.

The trajectory is the worship of heaven; it is celebration for the end to which creation is being brought. Indeed, it is the Father's will to restore all things in the well-beloved Son, the King of kings and the Lord of lords. The overtones are loud and clear in the Christmas Carols, and we see it when we penetrate beyond the first or second stanza. "It Came Upon the Midnight Clear . . ." pushes us to the days hastening . . . when the whole world gives back the song which the angels sing. The prayer is for the Holy Child of Bethlehem to "cast out our sin and enter in." In Joy to the World, the celebration is that "he comes to make his blessings flow far as the curse is found." And the Great Chorus echoes the praise from around the throne: "Hallelujah . . . for the Lord God omnipotent reigneth. The kingdoms of this world is become the kingdom of our Lord and of his Christ."

The prophets make no distinction between his coming as a baby in a manger and his coming as Lord to judge the world. The Spirit of the Lord would rest upon him, the spirit of counsel and might. He would not judge by the sight of his eyes or reprove by the hearing of his ears. He would smite the earth with the rod of his mouth, and with breath of his lips he would slay the wicked. Righteousness would be the girdle of his loins, and faithfulness the girdle of his raiment. They went on to say that during his reign, the lion shall lie down like the lamb; the suckling child will play over the hole of the asp. They will neither hurt nor destroy in all

God's holy mountain, for the earth shall be filled with the glory of God as the waters cover the sea.

The writer of Hebrews grasped the issue succinctly, making the distinction between the first and the second coming. The first coming was to bear the sins of many. He became sin, though he knew no sin. He suffered and died on the tree, enduring the curse of all who believe on his name.

The suppressed side of Christmas has to do with the two edges of the sword that goes forth from his mouth. It is a piercing sword. It pierced the heart of Mary, it pierced the side of Jesus, and it shall pierce the unrepentant ones who look upon him as their judge. Those who reject him join ranks with the soldiers who thrust him. But the piercing shall be reversed in the scenes of judgment when he comes with power, on the clouds of glory and with great majesty.

The soldier pierced him in his side, and out came the blood and water, opening a fountain for our cleansing. The crowd looked on, some jeering and mocking. But when he comes again there shall be no piercing of him; there shall be no mocking and jeering. He shall not come to be offered for sin; the offering has already been made. It is a full, perfect, and complete sacrifice. Rather, when he comes again, the piercing shall be reversed: Those who look upon him shall weep and wail because of him.

They shall look upon him whom they have pierced. The soldier did not act alone when he pierced him. No this is the joint effort of all who refuse to call on his name for salvation. Yea, this is the shame of the apostle for not heeding the call of the gospel without the death of Steven. Neither did the centurion speak only for himself when he looked upon him and cried, "Surely this is the Son of God." The scenes of the crucifixion shall be reversed. For then not only the centurion but all the world shall confess him. The sword that pierced him shall be the sword of judgment coming forth from his mouth, and with it he shall slay the wicked.

The sin not covered by his blood shall rise to condemn us. Yea, it shall be like a sword to cut us asunder. For he will not be the Savior to pardon. He will be the judge of those who are not justified by his blood. Fallen angels have already been judged and cast into infernal chains.

O the ways we pierce him. We pierce him as a nation when we forget God. We pierce him when we order the world in ways that leave out his justice, through oppression of the poor. We pierce him when we, make war against the weak, leaving the starving ones to fend for themselves.

We pierce him when we sell guns to the warlords and fill the streets with assault weapons. We pierce him when we turn away the hungry and leave the homeless out in the cold. We pierce him when we turn the house of prayer into a wrestling ring for our egos. This is not to so much as mention the countless sins of the flesh that result from passions that have not been laid on the altar of sacrifice.

But when he comes all uncovered commission and omission shall pierce us. I want to see him, look upon his face, and hear him say, "Come ye blessed of my Father. . . ." I want to behold his face in peace.

The first coming was as a baby in a manger. He was born to a virgin named Mary. The Spirit prepared the body for his obedience, that he might bear the sin of many. The second coming is for those who believe and trust him for salvation. At his coming the cry will go forth, "Go ye out to meet him. . . ." Some will be ready, having oil in their vessels, with their lambs trimmed and burning. Others who have neglected to take a supply of oil will hear the door shut in their face.

He is coming for a church without spot or wrinkle or any such thing. His salvation is for those who are looking and waiting for his appearance. He shall not come to bless our empires, but as the one to whom all thrones and kingdoms must bow. Things in heaven and in earth must confess that he is Lord to the glory of God the Father.

The sky shall unfold preparing his entrance; the stars shall applaud Him with thunders of praise. The sweet light in His eyes shall enhance those awaiting; And we shall behold him then face to face.

The angel shall sound the shout of his coming. The sleeping shall rise from their slumbering place, and those who remain shall be changed in a moment; and we shall behold him then face to face.

We shall behold him. . . . Face to face in all his glory. . . . Yes, we shall behold him our Savior and Lord.

seven RICHES FROM THE MANGER

For there is no difference between the Jew and the Greek: for the same Lord over all is rich unto all that call upon him. For whosoever shall call upon the name of the Lord shall be saved (Rom 10:12–13).

For ye know the grace of our Lord Jesus Christ, that, though he was rich, yet for your sakes he became poor, that ye through his poverty might be rich (2 Cor 8:9).

Today is the Fourth Sunday of Advent—frequently referred to as Christmas Sunday. Advent is a time of preparation, but there is a thin, perforated line between right preparation and celebration—if, that is, there is any line at all. For no element in preparation is more important than clarity regarding the focus. This is particularly so when it comes to Christmas. Unless we are exceedingly careful, we will celebrate Christmas—the holiday, the cultural event, the season of festivities. But Christmas means the celebration of Christ—God's gift for the salvation of the world. And so the dilemma—whether to celebrate the celebration or the celebrity, whether to celebrate the season or the reason, whether to celebrate the occasion or the Savior. The manger helps us. There are riches that come from the manger.

The ease with which the focus is shifted can be illustrated by the way we sometimes designate the day. The Greek letter "Chi" came to be used in the ancient church as a symbol for Christ. It looks like the English letter X. So a shortened version of Christmas would appear as "Xmas." For not knowing that X stands for Chi, and Chi stands for Christ, one could easily miss the importance of Christ altogether, and the celebration is no more than an orgy of festivity. The option is as simple as who holds the definition of the first letter. Here we have the issue set squarely before us: what makes the time meaningful; what makes the celebration rich? Do we celebrate the season or the Savior? I declare that the riches are found in the manger.

How ironic that the celebration of Christmas would fix the focus on spending sprees, opulence, wealth, and material riches, when Jesus was born in a manger—a corncrib, in a barn. Yet the cultural celebration is a time of merchants' madness and crazy credit. I believe I heard somebody call the day after Thanksgiving "Black Friday." Struck by the symbolism, my ears perked up to see what was meant. They went on to say that many merchants look forward to that day to come out of the red and get in the black (economically speaking) for the whole year. After Christmas, some are able to take their vacations, spending weeks on their yachts. Such is the cash flow, while we sing, "Joy to the world the Lord is come."

Consider for a moment what impression one would get upon coming to this country from another era or a poverty-stricken region of the world: what do you suppose they could conclude about the meaning of Christmas? The trees, the lights, the excess can be staggering. No joke, there are some streets where you'd better be careful: the lights can mesmerize you to the point of running off the road. I wonder what Joseph and Mary would think of how we celebrate, and what would the donkey say? I mean, it's almost like he had to take them to his house. Courtyard by Marriott, Holiday Inn and Best Western were full. They couldn't even get in an Econo-Lodge or Motel 6.

What if the celebration were indeed to focus on Christ, on poverty, on the manger? What if the accent shifted to what Jesus was sent to give—namely the salvation of his people from their sins? The apostle is telling us that if this is our focus, we find the true riches. In the manger, under the hay, down in the feeding trough, over behind the corn, down near the water: that is where the riches are to be found.

The context for this verse, which is our main focus, is the deep and explicit longing for his kinfolk to be saved. It is a passion that permeates the epistle. He has no shame in the matter. Rather, he is bold with his intention. The gospel is the power of God to salvation, to the Jew first, and also to the Greek. What comes to mind when looking at the pathos and drama involved is that of persons in search of what has been given in abundance, but they have overlooked it. What is longed for and desired has been left, like a will that remains sealed, like a bank account for which one does not have the number, like treasure in a box for which the key has been lost. The apostle testifies from what he knows: confess with your mouth the Lord Jesus; believe with your heart that God raised him. He has already descended: he was born in a manger. Nobody has been excluded: the Lord is rich unto all who call upon him. Get your riches from the manger.

Wherever the gospel is heard as good news there is some reversal of our order. For the most part, we get it backwards. So we get stuck with violence, war, greed, strife and poverty in the face of plenty. With the incarnation of the Son we have the moment that gives the paradigm. The riches of glory are given up for the poverty of the manger so that we might be rich. The early church depicted this reversal through their interpretation of messianic Psalms, like Psalm 45. The scene the Son left is described in regal language. The atmosphere is punctuated with fragrances from the oil of gladness. The garments smell like some mixture of myrrh, aloes, and cassia. The garments are glorious. The palace is accented with ivory. The poet put the pen to the page, saying, "My Lord has garments so wondrous fine, / and myrrh their texture fills; / . . . Out of the ivory palaces / into a world of woe; / only his great eternal love / made my Savior go."[1] And where did he go? He went to the backside of a barn in Bethlehem to deposit riches in a manger.

The scenes of glory are of brilliance—of resplendent light and beauty. Moses gets a glimpse from the mountain; Isaiah peers into the scene in the moment of his calling; Ezekiel sees the likeness of the glory in the Throne Chariot. The description is of riches beyond comparison. The Biltmore House would be a shack. So would the Vatican. Don't mention our little tabernacle. As the apostle put the matter on another occasion, the grace of our Lord Jesus Christ is seen in that "though he was rich, for your sakes he became poor, that ye through his poverty might be rich." In him we see the stripping of his divine nature and the emptying of himself into the body of a Galilean Jew. All the signs of his royalty are set aside to become like a homeless beggar, a wandering teacher—a prophet who healed lepers by touching them, a castaway who ate with tax collectors, harlots, and assorted sinners.

---

1. These are lines from Henry Barraclough's hymn, "Ivory Palaces," 1915.

You can celebrate Christmas by simply going with the flow. But to celebrate Christ there must be a reversal. I was listening to a commercial the other day, where the automaker was showing off the variety of vehicles that can be purchased at the dealership. The song they were singing said, "have a happy Honda Day." And a commentator was trying to come up with one word that rolls all the holidays into one. But to celebrate Christ one must go in reverse. The riches are located where they were put—not by accident, not as a matter of chance, not because the innkeeper was mean. The barn is where the Father sent the Son; the riches are in the manger.

Reversal, reversal: that's what salvation is all about. It is about repenting; turning around, and going where divine riches are given. Jews and Greeks get their riches from the same Lord. It makes no difference what the denomination or the division, the Lord Jesus born in the manger is the one we must serve. We will learn that in the church before the Lord changes. The question is whether we will celebrate ourselves or our Savior, whether we will celebrate our differences or our divine head. The celebration of Christ is finding the riches where the Father has placed them.

Looking to Jesus is oh-so-valuable for seeing where to locate the riches. It is possible for us to become so traumatized by poverty as the world defines it that we actually make ourselves poor—slaves to our material possessions, slaves to our toys, slaves to our debts, slaves to our selves. Mind you, this is not some pious platitude to tell the poor they should be content, when a few blocks from their squalor they can see the rich frolicking in their wealth. No, if we have a word for the poor it is to be accompanied by food and prophetic advocacy. Both observation and testimony disclose that countless numbers of those with silver and gold are imprisoned in deep poverty for not getting up, going in the direction of the shepherds, and finding the riches in the manger.

We will miss some of the greatest riches for not knowing where they are located. The characters given to narrate the birth of Jesus are ever so instructive in this regard. Before Gabriel appeared to Mary, he appeared to Zacharias the priest, the husband of Elizabeth who was Mary's cousin. They were both advanced in years, but the promise was that Elizabeth would bear a son who would turn the hearts of the fathers and the children to the wisdom of the just. The name of the son was to be John. But because Zacharias could not believe, he was struck with dumbness till the child was born.

The pattern has already started with the priest. For truly there are riches in silence, when no voice can be heard but the voice of God, and when there is no word but his. There is a stillness through which he can speak in the absence of the phone, email, and visitors. There is a preparation for receiving the riches of the Lord that requires the sealing of the lips until God bids us speak. Actually, the priests of God have nothing to say before receiving the riches that are given in silence.

Look, if you will, at how the celebration of Christ locates the riches. Listen to the young maiden named Mary to whom the angel Gabriel appeared. When he told her that she had found favor with God, and she had been chosen as the mother of the Lord, she couldn't believe her ears. She wanted to know how it could be. She knew the humble state of her abode and that her shadow had not darkened the door of a palace. Her betrothal was to a devout and humble carpenter, but they had not yet known one another. Gabriel informed her that he already knew the details she was disclosing; that's why she was chosen. Neither she nor any man could take credit for where God had decided to deposit the riches.

When she submitted and said, "so let it be," her soul began to magnify the Lord for showing the strength of his hand. With opened eyes, she could see the Lord scattering the proud in the imagination of their hearts and putting down the mighty. O the great reversal: for the Lord exalted them of low degree. He fills the hungry with good things and sends the rich away empty. Do you want your soul to magnify the Lord? Then say, "let it be with me according to your word" (Luke 1:38b).

Elizabeth was the witness Mary needed. When the riches were deposited in her, she could not broadcast. Friends her age would not understand. No doubt there was a space of time when she could not tell Joseph. But God was doing a corresponding work within Elizabeth. When Mary entered her presence the baby leaped in her womb, and she was filled with the Holy Ghost. The wisdom of her years and her walk with God endowed Elizabeth to give confirmation. Who knows the treasure that lies under-used for failure to receive the witness from the one in whom the Spirit has implanted it?

Only by God's preparation was Joseph able to consent to God's choice of where to locate the riches. But known to God are all his works.

This just and devout man was the instrument of protection when the jealous king began to rage and sentence all babies born in the frame of time surrounding Jesus' birth.

The Lord is rich toward those who call on him. The riches are now available, so that none need to ascend to bring Christ down. Wherever he is present, there is glory. The glory does not derive from the container of the riches, but whatever serves as the place of deposit does participate in the glory. On that cold night, in that barn behind the inn, the manger was transformed into an item of glory as it received the riches of heaven.

It must have been a struggle for Mary and Joseph. It may even be that they delayed their trip in hopes the child would be born before they commenced the journey. They had to go, for Augustus had decreed that all the world be taxed. Joseph and Mary were living in the northern province of Galilee, but Joseph was a descendant of Judah—from the house and lineage of David. They traveled as long as they could that night. When it was obvious that delivery was close they tried to find a room. But they were turned aside. It may be that Joseph pleaded for use of the barn. Or maybe the donkey started walking that way. When the baby was born there was nothing present to wrap him with but the cloth used to rub down the animals; yet on this occasion, that had to do. She named him Jesus, just as the angel had instructed Joseph. Lo and behold when she laid him in the manger it began to radiate with the glory of God, and a corresponding glory filled the sky as a star to brighten the heavens.

Shepherds in the field saw the glory. It was night, but the glory of the Lord shone all around them. The angel spoke to allay their fear, saying, "Unto you is born this day a Savior which is Christ the Lord." The sign was that they would find the baby wrapped in swaddling clothes lying in a manger.

The star appeared to Wise Men in the East. They were students of the stars, so they knew this was no ordinary occurrence. They made preparation for the trip, but not before they took gifts fit for a king. In a cryptic way, the gifts they carried revealed the riches God had deposited in that manger. They carried gold, a present fit for a king. They carried frankincense, the incense used by the priest. They carried myrrh, the bitter perfume used for burial. The poet summarized the gifts and their meaning, as by faith he overheard them sing, "Star of wonder, star of night, star with royal beauty bright; westward leading still proceeding, guide us to thy perfect light."

But look what happens. They followed the star only so far. It did not occur to them that the king they were seeking would be in a barn. So rather than following where the star was leading, they decided to stop by the palace to inquire of Herod. They did not know that this king had left the ivory palaces of glory for a barn, to deposit riches in a manger. They thought they were doing something noble when they departed from the star. All they did was trouble the heart of the king. He called his wise men, and when they read the scripture they found the very city where the star was leading. Only when they left the palace did the star reappear to lead them. The star drew nigh to the northwest, and over Bethlehem it took its rest. And there it did both stop and stay right over the place where Jesus lay. And where was the place? It was a manger, in a barn. But that's where God deposited the riches.

The riches are in the manger, the feeding place for the animals. The riches are in the barn, where the lowly traveler is found. The riches are in the places Jesus frequents, among those whom he befriends. The glory descends when we celebrate the Christ and witness with joy where God has chosen to be present.

It was the innkeepers oversight, but God's choice. It was Caesar's decree, but heaven's gift. I pray my decisions will be better, but I'm glad they turned him away. Herod might not let me in the palace. Caesar wouldn't have time for me. But I can make it to a barn. They turned Mary and Joseph away from the inn, and that's what made the glory manger.

And if I worship him, serve and obey him, one day he will take me to mansions he has prepared in his Father's House.

eight　EMANCIPATING THE PROCLAMATION

For there is no difference between the Jew and the Greek: for the same Lord over all is rich unto all that call upon him. For whosoever shall call upon the name of the Lord shall be saved. How then shall they call on him in whom they have not believed? And how shall they believe in him of whom they have not heard? And how shall they hear without a preacher? (Rom 10:12–14).

Here we are, a few days removed—or so it seems—from last year's Watch night. It seems to me that not so long ago we were on the threshold of last year. Is it just me who has that sense of time? I was speaking with a brother the other day in his nineties who said that the longer you live the faster the time seems to go. It would seem that it would be slowing down, but alas the testimonies are to the contrary. What trials have we known? What conflicts have we seen? What sorrows have we shared? But alas, what joys have joined our hearts? What blessings have bound our hearts together? There have been victories, healings, and deliverances from the hand of our God.

Truly, we are poised at the precipice of a moment of remembrance, a time for thanksgiving, a point fit for reorientation and clarification. Fresh perspective comes to us for pondering why we engage in this peculiar practice of worshipping God as the old year passes, while others are anticipating the artificial lightning of the skies, or touching the cups containing their spirits while they sing Auld Lang Syne. Sons and daughters of Africa removed to these shores who worshipped the Father of the Lord Jesus set a pattern some one hundred forty-one years ago as they prayed through the night. They waited for the same God who had saved them from their sins to sunder the chains of their bondage. In so doing they have given a gift to the church. It is a gift to all who would be bothered by the story of their deliverance. Alas, it is a summons to emancipate the Proclamation.

President Lincoln had drafted a proclamation granting emancipation to slaves in states, counties, and parishes in rebellion against the United States on the first day of the year of our Lord, one thousand eight hundred sixty-three. Great pressure had been brought to bear upon him to take this action. African American clergy and others who believed in liberty for all God's children urged the act, but they were not sure what the vacillating president would do. So they did what saints of God have done in every age as they waited for the divine hand to move. They prayed and kept vigil. That was a night of watching. Amid the currents of historical forces, they focused their attention on what God was doing. Those engaged in military conflict and possessing temporal power were at war. Those engaged in prayer anticipated the words of C. A. Tindley, who later declared, "There is a God who rules above with hand of power and heart of love; and if I'm right he'll fight my battle; I shall be free someday."[1]

The narrative of bondage is not told so often in this day as it once was told. Some say it is a history that belongs in the past, and it needs to remain past. Others prefer not to have the stain of slavery on their identity: they prefer not to be troubled by the sins of their fathers; or they believe their achievement has propelled them beyond the necessity of such a memory. But there are grave dangers in forgetting that in this land human beings were sold like livestock, that they were treated as property, and that religious ones debated whether they were beasts who did not possess souls. The spirit of bondage can outlive both the captive and the captor. But more, there are eternal lessons to be learned from those who saw the light of a new dawn before day broke and awaited it eagerly in prayer. Their faith teaches the virtue of emancipating the proclamation.

Believe me, there is a new bondage that threatens this land. It threatens captivity not only for the nation, but for the church. This is deep spiritual bondage from which none are spared because of their category. In spite of our historical sensitivities to bondage, African Americans are as susceptible as anyone else. This slavery is about more than color or racial designation. Indeed, there is a preoccupation with race and color that contributes to the blindness. Naming ourselves Christian, and modifying

---

1. From Tindley's hymn, "Beams of Heaven," ca. 1906.

the designation with the adjective "evangelical" is no inoculation. There is a blindness that threatens to make us ignore the bondage of those whom we designate as Others. Then we drink the inebriating nectars of ideologies that promote programs of bondage and dehumanization in the name of progress, or programs that extend a form of liberty that requires the servitude of another. The lesson we need is that of emancipating the proclamation.

The proclamation, of which Lincoln's emancipation was but a faint echo, is tucked in this passage that stares us in the face. It is wrapped up in the logic of this gospel account that tells us how we believe on the Lord Jesus for salvation. This is more than the feeble repetition of words. No, the Spirit puts the words in the mouth, and correspondingly inscribes them in the heart. This gracious act of God sweeps one into the divine will, where communion is afforded and obedience is wrought in the heart. What we have here is a translation into another domain. Here one knows what God has decreed, even if one must wait for history to catch up with the truth. Any split between political, economic, or social dimensions of emancipation from the comprehensive work of the Spirit of liberty yields a fragmented version, from which all human proclamations need emancipation. There is no difference between Jew and Greek in the need for salvation. Neither have we escaped the corruption of bondage we share with the creature without the emancipation of the True Master.

Follow me for a few moments, if you will. Slavery in the nineteenth century and before was rooted in the matrix of the so-called world where God had created some to be masters and some to be slaves. From that fabrication was derived the fiction of race, which located Africans and those of dark hue on the low end of the great chain of being. Africans were said to be descendants of Ham, and their destiny was to be hewers of wood and drawers of water. This was an eternal decree that was not to be violated. Struggles for liberty were sins against God. So much as the thought of mixing the races had to have its origin in sin. This led to a reign of terror, where it was said a black man had no rights that a white man was bound to respect.

The preaching of such a gospel (which was no good news at all) led to some of the bloodiest conflict known in the annals of human history. Brother fought brother, and the land was soaked in blood. So even with its flaws and limitations, the proclamation of Lincoln broke with a vicious and pernicious social philosophy, for he dared to advance the notion that all men—without exception—are created equal. That is an echo of the gospel, which is the true proclamation of emancipation.

The deepest crisis of the 1860s was that the church was not in a position to speak with one voice. It had no uniform word in the matter of whether a nation could survive half slave and half free. The major Protestant denominations had already split over the matter. They led the way to separation, and supplied much of the rationale for formal secession. African American preachers, and some others taking the same prophetic stance, proclaimed that God is the first pleader of the slave's cause, and for this horrid evil has brought down the greatest empires. One prophet dared to declare that if the preachers of the gospel would proclaim the truth for one Sunday, the evil institution would at once crumble. They pushed the president in a corner. Even with his proclamation, it took amendments of the constitution to outlaw slavery. He did not free slaves under his control. Yet these believers who watched and prayed through the night declared that God had spoken from Washington DC.

What is needed as we stand on the threshold of a New Year is the emancipation of the proclamation. This proclamation is not Lincoln's; it's the Lord's. We cannot believe on him for salvation if we have not heard him. We have not heard him till we emancipate his proclamation from the echo chambers in which we have allowed it to land. We are not saved because laws banning slavery and discrimination are on the books. Those with a design to keep people bound can find ways to do it. The ceremonial proclamation of a dead president cannot bind broken hearts or heal curses that run to three and four generations. Neither can laws calm the raging in the spirit that addicts a generation to drugs, violence, vulgar music, and countless acts of degradation.

The proclamation needs emancipation from those who jabber about being saved as if it is disconnected from the groaning of creation. No, the hope in which we are saved puts a tension between us and the creation that awaits its deliverance. The Spirit removes the scales from the eyes, exposing the hurt, the misery, the pain, and the suffering of this world that God has not ceased to love. It releases the gospel from the fetters of those who would take a quick trip to heaven and leave this suffering world behind. It's about more than the right position on gay marriage, abortion, prayer in the schools, and whether one says "under God" in the Pledge of Allegiance.

Let this New Year be an emancipation of the proclamation. The face of slavery has changed, and the new threat is the bondage of the gospel. The loss of old industry and agricultural staples leaves huge regions of the country in dire poverty. Whole sectors of the economy are closed to those who don't have the key to entry, and thousands of our boys and girls do not have a clue. Jobs going to immigrants, and industry being taken to countries where labor is cheap, is leading people to despair. The pattern is not limited to blue collar work; highly skilled, white-collar jobs are in the mix as well. The suppression of industry that kept wages low has led to depression in some rural areas. The gospel of salvation cannot be without regard to human need.

A worthy prayer for a New Year is, "Lord, emancipate your proclamation." See, there is great confusion in the land between the American way of life, democracy, and Christianity. It has led us into preemptive war from which no end is in sight. It has hardened the government to lie about the numbers needed, the readiness of troops, and the death of its children. We have met the terror of non-states with the terror of the state. The destruction of states strengthens the zeal of warriors in the non-states. Without the emancipation of the proclamation we will do it all in the name of a Christian state, causing the world to despise the God on whom we call.

The real truth is that the spirit of slavery has not been purged from the land that has never repented. No, the spirit of bondage is like a virus that mutates. The calling of the church is to be on guard for its reappearance in another guise. It can show up even within those who were once oppressed. The face of bondage has changed. It is no longer racial as it was in Lincoln's day. Purveyors come in all shades and hues. When the proclamation is emancipated it reiterates the words of this text: there is no difference between Jew and Greek. The same Lord is rich unto all that call upon him. The powerful need to be saved just like the weak; the rich need Jesus like the poor.

We are swiftly taking on the proportions and manners of an empire, as was the case with Rome in Late Antiquity. There was one nation against the world, or one nation ruling the world. It spread its army wherever it went; it denounced as criminal any who refused to yield; it declared its authority to arrest and to establish rulers who were loyal to the empire. Then the empire ran headlong into Jesus of Nazareth. They crucified him, but on the tree he crossed them up. Those who believed on him posed a threat that could not be contained. When he rose the battle was on sure 'nough. The empire managed to get the blessing of the church, and as a result the proclamation was muted. The church has been struggling ever since to emancipate its message from the empire.

The clock is about to strike midnight. A new year is about to break forth. Let the proclamation be emancipated. God wants to save us; he yearns zealously over us. Ready or not, he will redeem the world. The work of redemption will begin in the church. Ever so often he lets us see who we are without him. A storm passing from the ocean over land, and the state of Florida could have been gone. A tremor in the earth and South Asia is devastated: it makes our wars look like silly child's play. He calls for wars to cease. Does it take more? Do we think we are more righteous than those who perished? If we didn't know we needed him before, we surely should know it by now.

Let the proclamation be emancipated.

nine TIDINGS OF GOOD THINGS

And how shall they preach, except they be sent? As it is written, How beautiful are the feet of them that preach the gospel of peace, and bring glad tidings of good things? (Rom 10:15).

Where does a new year start for the believer? Does it start at Times Square with the dropping of the Ball? If so, there will be many who miss it. I would be the first one, for I was in the House of My God. Does it start with the party and the Big Bash? If so, that may be but an extension of the old year—just some more Fa La La. . . . A marvelous clue is given in the Good News tucked toward the end of the wonderful treatise on salvation in Romans 10. There is hardly a better place to start the New Year than with the gospel of peace, of glad tidings, of good things.

On Monday nights the game comes on with a question that is itself a form of celebration. The exciting question of invitation is, "Are you ready for some football?" A diehard fan is dressed up and ready to frolic, leaving no question as to what the answer is. I mean, Monday night is for the faithful, tried and true. After Sunday evening they want more. Well, the question I want to know on this first Sunday of the New Year, the second Sunday after Christmas is, "Are you ready for tidings of good things?" That's where the New Year starts.

For the church a New Year is another day in the Year of Our Lord, the year of our God's favor. The New Year starts with God, not with recycled news from last year, not with a rehearsal of what went wrong, what I don't like, or my complaints. It is not an eraser of memory, a revision of history, or a glossing over of what caused pain. No, it is a moment of thanksgiving. As mothers and fathers used to sing, "It was Jesus who brought me all the way, and he carried my burdens every day."[1] Yes, there were disappointments; yes, there were those who did what they should not have done. Some of what took place last year was totally unnecessary. There was war in the world and conflict in the city. But we dare to stop, to hark, to hear the herald who brings tidings of good things. We even go so far as to declare the feet to be beautiful.

For the Apostle Paul, soteriology (or the logic of salvation) is bound up with the preaching of the gospel. Yes, there were occasions on which he was willing to debate, but he did not really trust this form of communication for bringing on conviction and salvation. There was even an occasion on which he boasted, to demonstrate to those challenging his apostleship that they really had nothing on him. He even low-rated himself to highlight the grace that was extended when he was rescued. But when it comes to salvation—new life, new beginning, the accent that is to mark the consciousness of the heirs of God—there is no substitute for direct proclamation.

When you get to the core of the matter there must be conviction: a heart that believes because a word has come forth from a preacher who believes. There is no difference between Jew and Greek; everyone must call on the name of the Lord, and those who call shall be saved. The calling to which he has reference is not self-initiated: both the confession of the lips and the believing of the heart are the work of the Spirit. The word of faith is proclaimed by the preacher, who cannot preach without being sent. Then he gets carried away—all the way back to the exultations of Isaiah who said that even the feet of a sent preacher are beautiful.

Let's not start the year with a debate. How about if we save the survey for another time? Leave the opinion polls, the call-ins, and the write-ins for another moment. Start this year with me, with the preaching of tidings of good things.

The situation to which Paul takes us in his exultation is similar to our standpoint at the dawning of this year. In his sanctified imagination, he situates himself with the prophecy of Isaiah 52. By faith, the prophet sees the return of captives. He lifts his voice as herald bringing the tidings. He sees the release of captives from Egypt and Assyria, yet he speaks to those about to return from Babylon. What he is proclaiming is the

---

1. The quote is from a spiritual song known to the present author only by memory.

restoring power of God, the priority of what God has decreed, and he dares to make his utterance without shame or equivocation.

He takes up the vocation of the herald in a manner that forces us to appreciate it. The herald speaks to a city—to a people who have lost their spirit. They have been down so long they do not know how to look up; so many hopes have been dashed they have lost the very capacity. The word is uttered specifically to Zion, the holy city, but it is to all the people of God. He appears as one who travels from town to town to proclaim liberty, and to say that the bondage has ended. People whose necks have passed from one yoke to another are told they are no longer slaves; there are no foreigners to whom they must bow.

Feet shod, these heralds had to be ready to go anywhere. Every road was not easy. As a matter of fact, the image here is of a herald making a trip through the mountains. Such a venture could not be made without preparation for carrying the gospel. Protection was needed from rocks and adders. Since most travelers had no footwear but sandals, feet could be dirty and grimy. But because of the message they brought, even the feet were said to be beautiful.

Here is a herald who cannot be hindered. He epitomizes what it means to preach. More than all else, it is a call to awake and to put on one's strength. This is strength that is forfeited in slumber. The frame is present, the potential is there, the same mass and muscles exist, but sleep nullifies it all. The herald acts for God, who will not wait any longer. By the Spirit, the inertia is broken, and the silence comes to an end. It is God saying, enough of the lethargy. Tyranny and bondage have reigned long enough. It is God saying, "I am in spite of what you think you are . . . or are not."

The word of the preacher is a summons to shake off the dust and loose the bands from the neck. The word of deliverance has come; one need not remain a captive. Break forth in joy. This is not a word reserved only for one holding a specific office. Once the herald has spoken and been believed, the word can then spread like wildfire. His tidings were authorized. Remember, we are not talking about the day of satellites, the internet, or bloggers. We are not even talking about reporters, cameras, or radios. The herald was it. That's what made the feet so beautiful; once he had spoken and been believed, many could spread the tidings.

How beautiful are the feet! Heaven's herald has come. Indeed, the way was prepared for him by that prophet in the wilderness. There was a man sent from God whose name was John. He dressed in a girdle of camel's hair. He ate locusts and wild honey. He called the people to repent, for the kingdom of God was at hand. Multitudes went out to see him and were baptized in the Jordan. He was not the light; he was sent to bear witness to the light. He baptized with water; the herald coming after him would baptize with the Holy Ghost and with fire.

John saw him from a distance and hailed him, crying, "Behold the lamb of God that takes away the sin of the world." Heaven's herald requested to be baptized, and John's initial response was to refuse. He knew him from before his birth. Yea, he had witnessed from the womb of his mother Elizabeth, when she was filled with the Spirit and he leapt in her womb. The word of this herald was precious, for he came from the bosom of the Father. His was the word God's people had long awaited. They had walked in darkness and dwelled in the land of the shadow of death. The power of the witness was so great till the feet were beautified. John declared himself unworthy to unlatch the sandals on his feet.

How beautiful are the feet! Heaven's herald declared that the kingdom was at hand. The quenched Spirit had returned. In the form of a dove the Spirit came upon him and remained. With power from on high, he spoke without trepidation. The Spirit anointed him to preach good news to the poor, to heal the brokenhearted and the recovery of sight to the blind, to set at liberty those who were bruised, and to proclaim the acceptable year of the Lord. This is a proactive work that imparts faith into the hearts of those who do not reject him. It lifts the bowed down head and strengthens the feeble knee.

Heaven's herald has come. He proclaimed good news upon the mountain. He proclaimed good news beside the sea. He preached to multitudes in the wilderness. He was glorified on the mountain of transfiguration, and he preached from the tree; for he had declared that if I be lifted up from the earth I will draw all men unto me. Now that he has brought the news he was sent to proclaim, the tidings can be spread near and far.

And what are the tidings we have to bear in this New Year? With what news do we come before the people of God? Disappointment of disappointments for those who are looking for a new message: There is not another gospel. No, the story is the same. It is to be told with renewed vigor. And what are the tidings? The tidings are, "Thy God reigneth!" Now the watchmen can lift up their voices together, for in the matter of tidings we see eye to eye.

The tidings are that Our God reigns, no matter what the outcome of elections. In one county, ballots were lost, and the election must be held again. But the tidings are the same. In a few days there shall be an inauguration of the president elect. For some it will be a gala affair; for others it will be a day of sadness, and some will even protest. But the tidings are still the same. Thy God reigneth.

We live in a world that is in desperate need of tidings of good things. But before the world can hear the tidings, the church must believe what it has been sent to give. We must believe our herald. In this day as never before the children of God must learn afresh to believe the Report of the Lord. Priority must be given to what God has done, what doors he has opened for our faithful service, what provisions have been made for our righteousness and obedience. It is a biased word. It is a word that has already pre-judged what is good. It is a word that has already proclaimed victory.

Thank God for tidings of good things. We are free from the spirit that was expressed in the jingle they used to sing on Hee Haw. It went like this: "Gloom, despair, and agony on me; deep dark depression, excessive misery; if it weren't for bad luck I'd have no luck at all. Gloom, despair, and agony on me."

But tidings of good things release us from gloom, despair, misery, and agony; they set us free from fear and pessimism. Tidings of good things emancipate us from heightened chauvinism, cockiness, and arrogance. They break the shackles of xenophobia, mean-spiritedness, and slothfulness. Tidings of good things declare what God is doing, and for that we cannot be slothful or grudging in our service. Because the tidings are about God, we cannot be lackluster in our praise. We can praise him in the morning; we can praise him in the evening; we can praise him when the sun goes down! We can praise him in the sunshine and the rain. . . .

I was watching the news the other day, just like you, to see the latest word on the Tsunami that struck in South Asia. They showed one resort city in Indonesia that had a population of some 300,000 people.

It was a beautiful sight to behold. The beaches and hotels were a picture of luxury. People from all over the world had taken this region for their playground. They said that some people worked for three months in the tourist season and had no need to work anymore for the rest of the year. One moment there was relaxation and pleasure; the next moment there was horror. Below the ocean floor a fault relaxed, and a wall of water as high as the buildings rushed upon the land. Rich tourists and poor local people perished together.

My heart went out, and so did my prayers. My contribution by way of the church is going as well. I watched reports on the relief efforts of the nations, and I listened to the charge that the United States is stingy. Secretary Powell bristled at such a thought being expressed, and so did the president. Since then the United States has increased its pledge by ten times.

As I watched the cooperation of the nations in face of so great a tragedy two thoughts filled my mind. First, I saw as never before how foolish and infantile war is alongside such an awesome display of power. Just like it happened in one place, so it can happen anywhere—in New York, in Washington, in Durham, in Los Angeles. God can allow a few plates in the earth to shift and we could all come to the same end.

Then I noticed how the nations of the world joined forces to battle the threat of starvation and plague that can follow in the wake of so many deaths. In Sri Lanka two warring factions worked together to provide relief. As I reflected on the Table, I asked myself, "Could it be that we are being forced to bear good tidings through the shaking of the foundations?" What a moment for the church to hear her herald and proclaim tidings of good things!

Thank God for the Table. It is the sign beyond all others of where we both start and finish in the Year of our Lord. It is the reminder that when all is said and done the tidings are what God has done for the world.

The Table is a command to do what must follow when we believe the feet of our Herald are beautiful. Mary Thompson instructed:

> O Zion haste, thy mission high fulfilling,
> to tell to all the world that God is Light;
> that He who made all nations is not willing
> one soul should perish, lost in shades of night.

Behold how many thousands still are lying
bound in the darksome prison house of sin,
with none to tell them of the Savior's dying
or of the life He died for them to win.

Proclaim to ev'ry people, tongue and nation
that God in whom they live and move is Love;
tell how he stooped to save His lost creation
and died on earth that man might live above.

Give of thy sons to bear the message glorious,
give of thy wealth to speed them on their way;
pour out thy soul for them in prayer victorious,
and all thou spendest Jesus will repay.

Publish glad tidings, tidings of peace, tidings of Jesus—redemption and release.[2]

---

2. Mary Thompson, "O Zion Haste," 1871.

ten THE WORK OF FAITH

But they have not all obeyed the gospel. For Esaias saith, Lord, who hath believed our report? So then faith cometh by hearing, and hearing by the word of God (Rom 10:16–17).

Today is the First Sunday of Epiphany—the season after Christmas when we celebrate the appearance of the Lord. He came as a baby born in a manger; he came down through forty-two generations; he took upon himself the form of a servant. He did not remain incognito. Luke tells us that when eight days had passed, he was circumcised like other Jewish boys, and he was named Jesus, as the angel had instructed before his conception. Faith had become sight in the word made flesh.

When the days of Mary's purification were completed, she and Joseph took the child to Jerusalem to present him to the Lord. Lo and behold, there was a man named Simeon—an old man. He was devout, the Holy Ghost was upon him, and he waited for the consolation of Israel. Simeon saw what only Mary and Joseph knew. The word was out: this was the child. Anna, who had not departed from the temple for some eighty years, but served God with fasting and prayers night and day, bore the same witness. The word was out, the report was given, the work of faith began. All who heard it were forced to believe or disbelieve. Faith works.

And so it is that the Epiphany of the Lord forces the issue. The work of God for the salvation of the world is out of the corner; it is out in the open. For this the church rejoices. We celebrate, until the time in the Christian Year called Lent, the appearance of the Lord—the public ministry, the preaching, the healing, the mighty signs of power that make God's work manifest in the world. We dare not exchange his glory for another, or credit his mighty acts to Beelzebub. No, the work of faith forces the issue. Who shall believe the report? The arm of the Lord has been revealed. Faith works. Let those who believe rejoice!

And yet, all have not believed; all have not obeyed the gospel. This is the great frustration—yea, heaviness—of the apostle. Indeed, he turns to the prophet Isaiah to make sense of the painful experience. It perplexed him that such good tidings could be rejected. He quotes the prophet frequently in this section, both to comprehend the dilemma of the deaf ear, and to comprehend the work of faith in the heart that believes. In spite of the law, the promises, and the covenants, some who should know have not believed the report.

Thank God for the Epiphany! Thank God for Jesus! Thank God he appeared and was made known. Praise Father, Son, and Holy Ghost that the benefit reaches down through the generations. Thank God for the apostle's report concerning how salvation comes. This is a good word for every believer to know. It is especially good for those who would win souls—which should be every one of us. This is indispensable armament when bringing a wanderer home. You can expand it into ten laws if you want, or twelve steps if necessary. But this word can be as simple as two steps: confess with your mouth the Lord Jesus, and believe with your heart that God raised him from the dead. But we have here in the verses before us the response to any who dispute whether they have sufficient faith. It closes the door on those looking for an excuse to disobey the gospel. Yes you can believe if you have heard! The faith we need to believe is given when we hear the gospel. Can we say together: "So then faith comes by hearing, and hearing by the word of God." Let those who believe this rejoice!

Faith comes by hearing, not by understanding, not by interrogation, not by dissection, not by analysis. The voice here is passive: that is, the first action is God's. God does something for us. God does something to us. God reaches us by the word. O yes, there is great understanding that follows faith. Indeed, one of the great teachers of the church declared that theology (reasoning about God, discerning the logic given in the word) is "faith seeking understanding." As we walk by faith we give steady and focused attention to the ergonomics of faith—that is, to how faith works. The first movement is work (*ergon*) upon the deadened spiritual sense—that is, the opening of the eyes, the loosening of the tongue, the unstopping of the deaf ear. You might not be able to explain it any more than the man who declared, "this one thing I know . . . whereas I was blind, now I see." But the same is so for those who formerly could not speak or hear.

By the Spirit, God moves first within the deepest realm, the tacit dimension, at the presuppositional level. This dimension, where faith is deposited, precedes instrumental knowledge. It makes no difference what the field of learning—before you can make arguments or proofs, you must assume something. You must accept the theory before you can make the proof. You must believe what you have is evidence before giving explanations or verifications. Faith is a donation; it is a gift. Faith comes by hearing, and hearing by the word of God.

We are not talking here about every careless trickle from the lips. The word is more than a string of letters or cute syllables. No, this is the word (the *rhema*) that is quick and powerful. It pierces to dividing asunder of flesh and spirit; it digs down into a clogged ear. It does not return void. This word passes through the ear canal, searches the heart, discerns the thoughts, discloses to us our objections to the truth and demolishes every high thing that exalts itself against the knowledge of God. It is extended to us by the very arm of the Lord. It performs a work that is far more than intellectual assent: it compels obedience.

Hearing, as we have it in this passage, can be compared to the vibration that takes place within the ear canal. The sound is like a little hammer, tapping on the drum. By a mystery that occurs within that chamber, which is described marvelously by science, the vibrations take on discrete meaning that is translated within the brain. Consider the wonder of hearing: I can transmit my thought to you by a sound generated in my voice box, and the ear can drum that meaning to your brain, with precision.

Africans have known for centuries how to make their drums talk, but communication is incomplete without the ear. Clever as they might be, iPods don't have anything on the ear. Without the ear there would be no use for them. But look in the spiritual ear: by means of preaching the very mind of God can be transmitted to my little brain. The hearing to which this text refers is more than clear reception: it prompts the response of obedience.

The point of origination is with the sender. Hence the question, "How can they preach unless they are sent?" The sending is in the Spirit: as the Father sent the Son, so the Son sends us. Our sending is accompanied by the effusion of the Holy Breath of the Risen Christ, who bids us, "Receive the Holy Spirit." Someone said that the molecules of his breath remain in the church. If that be, they saturate the word of one who is sent.

One might speak here of the ergonomics (the dynamic work) of faith within the spiritual ear. It breaks inertia, brings contemplation to an end, produces an inward movement into the will of God, and the work extends through the body in acts of obedience. We are purged of dead works. Faith itself is the work: it is a manifestation of the Spirit for one to say, "Lord, I believe." We know Christ abides by the Spirit that is given in these initial acts of confessing and believing. Here we are on the other side of grace. We are the recipients of divine capacitation.

Faith extends grace to the point where we are affected. We cross the threshold in motions of obedience. We come alive to God. In the language of the Covenant, we engage to walk in the Spirit. Paul and James were not as far apart as Luther thought: the ergonomics of faith dispense with dead works, replacing them with the Spirit's energy. This comes by hearing a word that will not return void. It can be disbelieved, but it cannot be met with indifference. There can be resistance and hardening. Even then there may be a performance that cannot be seen with the natural eye, or within the lifetime of the one who gives the utterance. Thank God for the very work of faith.

In the dynamics of faith one sees what I call the "ephphathatic" work of the Spirit that is not limited to the members, but that extends through the body of Christ. I am drawing here on the drama of how the Lord Jesus speaks into the deaf ear, causing it to open (Mark 7:34). He speaks the word "ephphatha"—which means, "be opened"—to create the capacity for hearing where it did not exist. They brought him one with a speech impediment and who was deaf. Jesus put his fingers into his ears, spit, and touched his tongue. Then he looked up to heaven and said to him, "Ephphatha, that is, Be opened." His tongue was loosed, and his ears were opened.

Have you ever had a clogged ear that left your hearing impaired? Sometimes the pressure of flying can be so great that not only can you feel it; you can't hear the person beside you. Isn't it wonderful when the ear pops? What if you had to stay like that? It might hurt, but it still feels good when it pops. What about wax? It can get so bad that you have to go to the doctor. She will put a solution down in the canal to dissolve that crystallized wax—and whatever else is down there. A Q-Tip is helpful for removing the gunk. Even worse is fluid or infection behind the drum.

Then they must puncture it to relieve the pressure and restore hearing. It hurts, but O what a relief it is. This is only impairment. Jesus comes to us when we are spiritually deaf.

Thank God for the ephphathatic work of the Spirit. This is where the Risen Christ speaks to the body, saying, "Be opened," and creates the capacity for hearing. There are limits on our obedience until he speaks by this power and it takes effect. There is work that must be done, but we will never rise in obedience until the ear of the church as a body is opened. Shrill voices may cry, but there is no hearing. The preacher is instructed to lift up his voice like a trumpet. But it takes the ephphathatic work of the Spirit upon the body for there to be hearing.

A ministry here, a ministry there, vitality over yonder is good. But it is not good enough. For those who have given themselves to the ministry of prayer, here is a worthy focus: learn to speak this word on behalf of the church—Ephphatha. On the lips of the Lord it is a command; on our lips it is prayer for God to open the ear of the church.

The work God has given the deacons could not come at a more timely moment. It is not enough for a small segment to hear from God; neither is it good enough for all hearing to be private. We will see a difference in the house when the ear of the body is opened. Let's pray earnestly for God to touch our ears severally and bring us into a common space to create that spiritual ear through which we can hear in common—in communion.

So don't mind me when I can't finish in twenty minutes. Some private sessions and telephone conversations are longer than that; the same is so in the time set aside for teaching. But there are times when the Lord desires to speak to the church—through one ear. The preacher can feel the spiritual ergonomics when the ear is closed; and God knows, you can feel it when they come open. We know the difference in praise: when the Spirit says, "Praise God" and the ear is open you don't need anybody to pump it up. That's the sort of praise that makes space for itself—whether doxology is written on the program makes no difference. The Lord willing, we are going to remove any hint of dichotomy between "Praise and Worship," as if there could be such a thing as worship without praise.

Ephphathatic work upon the body creates that common open ear. It reverses the impediment that prevents us from hearing one another. In more cases than not when we "ain't studdin' somebody" it is because we are not hearing them. God grant us to hear each other. God grant us to hear a cry and know what it means. God grant us hearing that does not go in one ear and out the other.

There is a generation that will not hear us, and that we will not hear until the Spirit creates that common ear. There is a moral noise pollution pervading our civilization that has effectively muted certain ethical sounds from the scale. There are frequencies that cannot so much as be heard. Some of them pertain to life, abundance, and spiritual blessing. It's almost like the situation many of us can remember when parents spoke, but we were preoccupied with our music, our sulking, or our daydreaming. They would shout and ask, "Are you hard of hearing?"

In our day a slap up side the head was sufficient cure. But even that will not work if the ear has not already been opened. Ephphathatic work is required where we are taken back to spiritual phonetics, and to the development of the vocabulary that trains the ear to respond to the things of God. This is an environment that is infused with prayer. Sometimes it requires feeding, hugging, and weeping. In the ether of such tenderness and love the Lord Jesus will loose stammering tongues, open blinded eyes, and ears will respond to his voice when he says, "Be open."

Faith works. It comes by hearing the word of God. It is necessary that the word be declared and heard. In the work that has been given it is crucial. For that cause, it is critical to know when the ear is stopped up, aching, or closed due to impairment. There are cries in our communities from persons with ear impairments. Some have been polluted by the confusing noises of this generation. Others are aching so badly that they can't hear a thing. God has called us to listen to the lambs, so we will know when they are crying from an earache.

You know, we really need to get back to bringing our children to Sunday school. Wednesday night is good; so is Messiah's House on the Second Sunday. But nothing takes the place of old fashioned Sunday School, where each week the word is placed in the ear. Really, this is like the finger of the Lord. Otherwise, you will live to regret that the ears have not opened. Spiritually speaking, they will grow up hard of hearing. God will be calling, and they will not know his voice from the bustling crowd and the rat race noise. Have you heard the record by Helen Baylor? She was delivered from drugs and alcohol while she was dying. But she had a praying grandmother. Somewhere along the line, she had learned to call on the name of Jesus.

Faith comes by hearing, and hearing by the word of God. As we walk with the Lord, nothing will prove to be more soothing to the ear than the sound of his word. The spiritual senses enfold around one another till one hardly knows whether it is a matter of seeing, tasting, or hearing. It is beautiful beyond measure to see the Savior taking you in his arms like a good and tender shepherd; there is no taste like the honey of the word. But thank God today for the sound of his voice. When you have heard his voice and it speak of his love, you long to hear it again. He speaks and the sound of his voice is so sweet that the birds hush their singing.

There is nothing like his voice, saying, "fear not, I have redeemed you . . . when you walk through the waters I will be with you. . . . He asked the children on one occasion, "Hast thou not known, hast thou not heard, the everlasting God. . . . He gives power to the faint. . . . They that wait upon the Lord" (cf. Isa 40:28–30, 43:1–6).

John said he was in the Spirit on the Lord's day (cf. Rev 1:9ff). He heard his voice like the rolling of many waters. I want to see him and look upon his face. But I also want to hear his voice. The same voice that called me to faith and salvation is the voice I want to hear at last. I want to hear my Lord say, "Well done."

eleven THE GOOD NEWS OF DIVINE PROVOCATION

But I say, Have they not heard? Yes verily, their sound went into all the earth, and their words unto the ends of the world. But I say, Did not Israel know? First Moses saith, I will provoke you to jealousy by them that are no people, and by a foolish nation I will anger you (Rom 10:18–19).

The most prominent theme of the gospel is, by far, glad tidings of good things. And just what are those good things? They are given to us in fine summary in this very chapter. The word of faith is near to us—on our lips, in our hearts. We do not have to ascend into heaven or bring him up from the grave. The glad tidings are that whosoever may call upon the name of the Lord shall be saved. Our God reigns. The good news is that faith comes by hearing, and hearing by the word of God. With the word comes the power of faith. Indeed, faith comes by hearing, and hearing by the word of God.

Still, there is a subtheme nearby. It is lurking not far away, but it remains in striking distance. It is articulated in the form of the question, "Have they not heard?" It is not that the word hasn't been uttered. As the psalmist put it in Psalm 19: there is no speech or language where the voice of the Lord is not heard; the line has gone out into all the world. Indeed, he begins that Psalm by affirming, "The heavens declare the glory of God, and the firmament shows his handiwork." All have not heard. The good news is accompanied often by this tragedy: all have not heard, and all have not believed the report. But God is not about to give up on those whom the Holy One has chosen, without further comment, without an additional contest. God reserves the prerogative to provoke the called in efforts to persuade them to come.

Romans 10 ends on the same note with which it began—with passion, with zeal. At the beginning of the chapter the zeal of Israel is not according to knowledge; at the end of the chapter the source of the zeal is divine provocation. This would make it consistent with the zeal of the Lord. We see God going to extreme measures to bring about hearing, so that the people might be saved. The first movement of God is proclamation; the second movement, which is likewise in love, is provocation. I want to talk about the Good News of Divine Provocation.

Anyone who has a child, or has been one, can relate well to this second movement; so that includes us all. The first movement is when Mom tells you—tells you what? Tells you to make up your bed, clean the kitchen, start the dishwasher, do your chores. The first movement is when she tells you. The second movement is when she tells you again, and usually this comes with consequences. The way of love is not to tell you once, and then to give up on you or the issue at hand. The lesson is too important. Even in old times, when the father's rule was, "I speak once," there was a second chance. The second movement might be with a switch or a strap, but the instruction was not allowed to drop. It was not in our interest for the good word to go unheeded.

On an occasion I spoke to one of my sons twice—after he was old enough to smell himself. I asked him if he knew what was meant by "fair warning." He said "No." I said, "I have told you twice; after this anything I do to you is fair." I gave him a break, but I could not let the issue go. For some, the second movement is accompanied by "put up your gameboy," "no playstation this afternoon," "give me the cell phone," "no DVD," or "you can't go out with your friends." The second movement is often easy to miss, because it is not about punishment: that is another movement—perhaps the third or fourth. The second movement is about something else: it is about being sure to get your attention; it is refusal to let a good word fall to the ground. This is what God did for Israel through the prophets and once again through the apostle in the dispensation of the gospel to the Gentiles. It was good news through an act of divine provocation.

The beauty in this word is that despite the sin of the nation, the rebellion of the masses, and rejection by the majority, God can and does continue to extend grace. God is not turned off the moment we turn away. Indeed, there are occasions when we feel like God has forsaken us, and really all that is involved is that we have turned from God. What we feel is but a provocation to return and be healed. There is an extension of grace through acts that make us jealous for what God desires to give and for the relation God desires to have in the first place. This is an expression of divine determination to bring forth the praise, the service, the obedience that corresponds to his love and purpose for us. There is good news in divine provocation.

The provocation to which the apostle has reference comes by means of those who were outside the commonwealth of Israel—those whom one would not expect to honor God; the foolish nation, as he puts it. We see instances of this where Abraham lies and says Sarah is his sister rather than his wife; but God troubles the heart of the pagan king who refuses to sin. Then there is the priest of Midian who fears God and teaches Moses how to judge the people. Rahab the harlot extends hospitality to Caleb and Joshua, Ruth the Moabitess refuses to leave Naomi, and Uriah the Hittite shows more loyalty to the commandments of God than King David.

God takes the faithfulness of the outsider to provoke the insider. It can be one from a different generation or category who sets the example, but the divine intention is to bring us to greater obedience. He can bring in one from the fields of sin and show us what true love for God looks like. He can take one who was shy to reveal the character of yielded praise. God can take the voices of the babies to show the pros how to sing. God can take the innocence of the beginner to provoke the veteran to seek deeper anointing and increased power. I don't care who you are, ever so often you see a purity of devotion, an inshining of the Spirit that can serve as provocation for greater devotion and unfeigned faith.

Mind you, I am not talking about jealousy of the sort that turns you against the one God is using. That can be counterproductive and spiritually lethal. That can cause us to harm a brother or sister, to stand in the way of God's plan, to undermine the good of the gospel. The truth is that no matter what God does through another, God's will for me is not diminished. No, this spiritual motion is to drive us to repentance, so we turn to receive what has been offered at God's hand. It is to disturb the state of rejection or halting.

Provoking to jealousy means stimulating to excite rivalry or fire zeal. God's intention is to cause us to feel a zeal for him that corresponds to the jealousy he has for us. This isn't the zeal that is not according to knowledge: zeal that led Paul and others to persecute Christians. Rather, God's purpose was to excite his people to do the work of the kingdom into which they had been called. It is to stimulate passion for righteousness that drives from within. This provocation is to perform in the manner Moses envisioned in Deut 32:21, where God says, "They have moved me to jealousy with that which is not God; they have provoked me to anger with their vanities: and I will move them to jealousy with those which are not a people; I will provoke them to anger with a foolish nation." See God's determination to draw them back? Passion is the key. Paul goes on to the scroll of Isaiah (chapter 65), where the same theme is pursued. The people of God's choice are rebellious, yet a nation that did not know his name found him.

He uses this sketch as a parallel for what God has done through the church. God has brought together people who were not formerly a nation. Sinners, believing Jews, Greeks, Gentiles, slaves, and those of every variety heard and responded to the gospel of Jesus Christ. But is this so the Jews might be cast out? By no means. It was to be a provocation to jealousy, so that they could take their rightful place.

There is great grace in being within the range of provocation—where the ear is still open, where there is still enough jealousy to inspire zeal. Don't get it in your mind to hurt anybody brother, but you want to feel at least a hint of jealousy when another man keeps showing interest in your wife. A sign of health is when another man's attention drives you back to your own. Children don't want even their friends to get so close to their parents that they are pushed out of place. You might be my friend, but that's my mother. Yes, you can take it too far, but there ought to be some point at which provocation makes us say, this is my church, my calling. I am not speaking here of pathological possessiveness; but it is a reminder of where we ought to be in God.

The apostle has taken us to the point where God is not shy in speaking of his passion. God is not portrayed here as some "cool dude" who is unbothered, indifferent. No, here God is saying, "Israel, you are the one I want, and I will not let you go. Now I want to know if you have any passion left for me." So God acts to stimulate, to stir up that zeal.

Remembering the life and ministry of Martin King in the church is celebration of divine provocation. It is the servant of the Lord, the prophet of the Most High speaking to the church and to a nation that claimed to fear God in a day when many had not heard. A word had been preached to inspire zeal that was not according to knowledge. In oh-so-many pulpits, the gospel of God had been perverted. For God's people of African descent, there was a conflicted word. For others who knew the racist lie, there was a choice to be made. There was a voice in the land calling for the overthrow of oppression, and the ways of violence and destruction were viewed as a viable option. Feeling the mood and restiveness of the people in the streets and on the farms, King cried to announce the provocation of God that was to stir the zeal of the lovers of God.

The question was whether the church would be provoked to jealousy, to a zeal for being the witness for which God called, or would she be content for the cry to come from another. It was a time for Christians to take sides. Not so long ago I was in the city of Memphis at the Civil Rights Museum. It was formerly known as the Loraine Motel where King spent his last night. The garbage workers of the city had struck, and King and his cohorts from the Southern Christian Leadership Conference had been called in for assistance. The Mass Meetings were being held at Mason Temple, the Tabernacle for the Church of God in Christ. On the balcony following his speech in defense of the poor and suffering of this land, King was felled by the assassin's bullet. Among all King said that night was, "I want to live a long time; longevity has its place. But I am not worried about that tonight; I just want to do God's will, and he has allowed me to go to the mountaintop."

As I walked through the Museum my mind roamed back to those days of segregation—riding the back of the buss, drinking from water fountains marked colored, and suffering untold indignities for the color of one's skin. We don't like to talk so much about it today. Mistakenly we often claim those times have passed. But the worst part of it all was the abominable claims that were made about God. Theologians and preachers lied to the people, claiming that God created superior and inferior races: that some were created to be masters and some were created to be slaves. They lied on God, claiming that darker races were created with less intelligence than the white master race, and that intellectual capacity could be measured by the angle of the forehead. Countless boys and girls had their brilliant futures stifled, and many a man and woman was turned into a beast of burden because the people of God held their peace.

A trial is under way in Mississippi now for a preacher named Killens, who is accused of ordering the murders of three young students, named Goodwin, Schwerner, Chaney. He is charged with giving the orders to kill them, after they had been followed by a mob that became angry because they registered black people to vote. The case came up before, but the jury was hung, because one woman could not vote to convict a preacher. Now after nearly fifty years, the papers of the States Sovereignty Commission are being opened, revealing the names of some 87,000 persons who were labeled criminals because they advocated an end to segregation. These papers include testimony from thousands of persons who knew the dark secret of who ordered killings, bombings, and burnings. The saddest part of it all is that so many of these persons described themselves as acting in the name of the Lord. They had mixed the message of the Ku Klux Klan with the gospel of Jesus Christ.

God stepped outside the religious establishment to find a prophet to provoke the church and the nation. Yes, King was a black Baptist preacher, and for black Baptists that is where the church begins and ends. But during that day all black churches were called sects. The scholars said that what black folk did was a feeble copy of historic Protestantism. One said that our worship was a form of frenzy, and another called it folk religion. So God said I will move outside the mainstream. I will find a servant of my preparation. I will provoke those who call my name to see if they have any jealousy to match the zeal I have for them. They were not in the majority, but thousands came pouring out of the churches to bear witness to the nation that We Shall Overcome, if in our hearts we do not yield. They did not say to what they must not yield. But I will declare the great danger to which we must not yield: it is an indifference to the way of God and the cry of the needy. For when we can no longer be provoked by God, there is no hope for us or for our world.

The story is told of one preacher in Durham who was put on trial for his involvement in the demonstrations. He was young, white, and somewhat brash. The district attorney decided to make an example of him. So he examined him sternly, charging him with being an outsider, coming in town to meddle. He asked him where he was from. His answer was that he was from Mississippi. That didn't advance the DA's point. He asked him whether he was a member of SNCC. He said No. He asked him whether he was a member of CORE, or the NAACP. The answer was

No. Then he asked whether he was a member of any organization that had as its avowed mission the ending of segregation. The young preacher said, Yes Sir. The DA asked what that institution was. The young preacher answered, "I belong to the Church of Jesus Christ," and the courtroom was brought to a hush.

As in the day of King, the church is being provoked by God to stimulate any jealousy for God that remains within us. By the crimes of the state, the trouble in the world, and the upheaval within nature, our passion is being put to the test.

BIBLIOGRAPHY

Broadus, John A. *On the Preparation and Delivery of Sermons*. 4th edition. San Francisco: Harper & Row, 1979.

Buber, Martin. *I and Thou*. A new translation with a prologue and notes by Walter Kaufmann. New York: Scribner, 1970.

Buttrick, David. *Homiletic: Moves and Structures*. Philadelphia: Fortress, 1987.

Cleland, James T. *Preaching to be Understood*. New York: Abingdon, 1965.

Craddock, Fred B. *Preaching*. Nashville, TN: Abingdon, 1985.

Davis, H. Grady. *Design for Preaching*. Philadelphia: Muhlenberg, 1958.

Hays, Richard B. "Exegesis." In *Concise Encyclopedia of Preaching*, edited by William H. Willimon and Richard A. Lischer, 122–28. Louisville, KY: Westminster John Knox, 1995.

Harris, James H. *The Word Made Plain: The Power and Promise of Preaching*. Minneapolis, MN: Fortress, 2004.

Johnson, James Weldon. *God's Trombones: Seven Negro Sermons in Verse*. New York: Penguin, 1990.

Jones, Lawrence Neal. *African Americans and the Christian Churches: 1619–1860*. Cleveland, OH: Pilgrim, 2007.

LaRue, Cleophus. *The Heart of Black Preaching*. Louisville, KY: Westminster John Knox, 2000.

Long, Charles H. *Significations: Signs, Symbols, and Images in the Interpretation of Religion*. Philadelphia: Fortress, 1986.

Long, Thomas G. *The Witness of Preaching*. Lousiville, KY: Westminster John Knox, 1989.

Lowry, Eugene L. *The Homiletical Plot: The Sermon As Narrative Art Form*. Expanded edition. Louisville, KY: Westminster John Knox, 2001.

Massey, James Earl. *Designing the Sermon: Order and Movement in Preaching*. Nashville, TN: Abingdon, 1980.

Mitchell, Henry H. *Black Preaching: the Recovery of A Powerful Art*. Nashvillen, TN: Abingdon, 1990.

Otto, Rudolf. *The Idea of the Holy: An Inquiry into the Non-Rational Factor in the Idea of the Divine and its Relation to the Rational*. Translated by John W. Harvey. London: Oxford University Press, 1970.

Polanyi, Michael. *The Tacit Dimension*. Gloucester, MA: Peter Smith, 1983.

Proctor, Samuel D. *The Certain Sound of the Trumpet: Crafting a Sermon of Authority*. Valley Forge, PA: Judson, 1994.

———. *"How Shall They Hear?": Effective Preaching for Vital Faith*. Valley Forge, PA: Judson, 1992.

Sernett, Milton C. *African-American Religious History: A Documentary Witness*. 2d ed. Durham, NC: Duke University Press, 1999.

Smith, H. Shelton, *In His Image, But . . . : Racism in Southern Religion, 1780–1910*. Durham, NC: Duke University Press, 1972.

Soulen, Richard N., and R. Kendall Soulen. *Handbook of Biblical Criticism*. Third edition. Louisville, KY: Westminster John Knox, 2001.

Stookey, Laurence Hull. *Calendar: Christ's Time for the Church*. Nashville, TN: Abingdon, 1996.

Taylor, Gardner C. *How Shall They Preach*. Elgin, IL: Progressive Baptist, 1977.

Tisdale, Leonara Tubbs. *Preaching as Local Theology and Folk Art*. Minneapolis, MN: Fortress, 1997.

Turner, William C. *The United Holy Church of America: A Study in Black Holiness Pentecostalism*. Piscataway, NJ: Gorgias, 2006.

Wink, Walter. *Engaging the Powers: Discernment and Resistance in a World of Domination*. Minneapolis: Fortress, 1992.

———. *Naming the Powers: The Language of Power in the New Testament*. Philadelphia: Fortress, 1984.

———. *Unmasking the Powers: The Invisible Forces that Determine Human Existence*. Philadelphia: Fortress, 1986.

www.ingramcontent.com/pod-product-compliance
Lightning Source LLC
Chambersburg PA
CBHW020857160426
43192CB00007B/960